D1484730

LOVE
THE JOB,
LOSE
THE STRESS

Successful Social and Emotional Learning in the Modern Music Classroom

LESLEY MOFFAT

Copyright © 2020 Lesley Moffat.

All rights reserved. No part of this publication may be reproduced, distributed, or transmitted in any form or by any means, including photocopying, recording, digital scanning, or other electronic or mechanical methods, without the prior written permission of the publisher, except in the case of brief quotations embodied in critical reviews and certain other noncommercial uses permitted by copyright law.

ISBN: 978-19-5-315310-4

Published by

LIFESTYLE
ENTREPRENEURS
P R E S S

If you are interested in publishing through Lifestyle Entrepreneurs Press, write to: *Publishing@LifestyleEntrepreneursPress.com*

Publications or foreign rights acquisition of our catalog books. Learn More: *www.LifestyleEntrepreneursPress.com*

Printed in the USA

Dedicated to
George H. Moffat
My soulmate, husband, and best friend.
Thank you for always believing in me.

You are not lucky.
You know what you are?
You are smart,
you are talented,
you take advantage of the opportunities that come
your way
and you work really, really hard.
I won't call you lucky.
I will call you a badass.
—Shonda Rhimes

Contents

My Gift to You. 1

Foreword 3

Introduction 7

Chapter 1: My Life's Work Is So Much More Than
Just a Job 11

Chapter 2: I Love My Job but It's Killing Me 20

Chapter 3: The Badass Band Director's Bible 34

Chapter 4: Step 1: The Moffat Music Teacher
Mojo Meter 41

Chapter 5: Step 2: Identifying the 3 C's:
Care, Clarity, and Consistency 50

Chapter 6: Step 3: Identifying Your Priorities. 67

Chapter 7: Step 4: SNaP Strategies
for Music Teachers 81

Chapter 8: Step 5: Tuning Our Bodies 103

Chapter 9: Step 6: Creating Your Own First Four
Minute Protocol. 129

Chapter 10: Coda 156

Chapter 11: Fine 174

Acknowledgments. 185

Thank You 187

About the Author. 189

My Gift to You

If you are looking for ways to help your physical and mental health, check out my first book, *I Love My Job but It's Killing Me* (free eBook at mPoweredEducator.com/freebook). In it, you'll find details of how I was able to turn my health around and stay in the job I dearly loved. That book has the tools and strategies you need for getting your personal wellbeing on track. This book is designed to help you take what you learned in the first book and use the strategies to up-level your teaching game.

Foreword

by Dr. Tim Lautzenheiser

Lesley Moffat's newest book, *Love the Job, Lose the Stress*, redefines the term "self-help." Her first best seller, *I Love My Job, but It's Killing Me*, awakened us to a new landscape of personal and professional sanity. This latest-greatest contribution offers a tried-and-true blueprint for vocational success while embracing the critical importance of fueling one's mental, emotional and physical health. Spot on! Bull's eye!

What is uniquely wonderful about Lesley's writing is based on her own teaching journey. Her wisdom reflects reality rather than hypothesis. She has "been to the well," she "walks her talk," and she does it with a sense of understanding unknown in common hours. Rather than simply focusing on the obvious, she delves into the why, what, and how of the given situations:

- Here's *why* you need to take stock of this concern or breakdown.
- This is *what* you can do to reset your compass to achieve resolution.
- ... and this is *how* you can do it to reach your destination.

A bit of history: By all standards, Lesley Moffat was at the top of her teaching (band directing) career. She developed a program-of-excellence recognized (and envied) by her colleagues. The numbers grew, the quality soared, and the awards continued to spotlight this one-of-a-kind culture-of-artistic-excellence being driven by her ongoing desire to serve the students, the school, and the community. However, all of this manifested at the expense of Lesley's health and well-being. To attain these high, self-appointed educational standards, she was short-changing the most important part of her program: *Lesley Moffat*. Let us be reminded of this cornerstone truth: "You can't lead others until you lead yourself." Fortunately, she recognized her plight and executed a massive course-correction. Now, we are the benefactors of her self-explored research via her trademark writing talents.

This manuscript is an endless treasure chest of immeasurable value. From the self-reflection templates to proven time-management skills, each page reveals yet another golden nugget you can integrate into your own daily agenda. This is not a book you read and then put on the shelf; rather it is a file cabinet of priceless data certain to bolster the health, happiness and good fortune of every (music) educator.

We've all heard the familiar teacher outcry, "I'm tired. I'm frustrated. My health is suffering. I live in stress. I don't have a life. I don't know what to do. I want to give-up. *I'm just plain burnt out!*" It truly is "a sad state of affairs" when one experiences this kind of desperation. Might I suggest that reading *Love the Job, Lose the Stress* offers-up a powerful prescription availing us to a personal/professional avenue arriving at one's desired contentment and fulfillment.

Lesley, *thank you!* We know the master teachers are also keystone role models. That being said, *you* are an exemplar for all of us!

Introduction

I completed the first draft of this manuscript on March 3, 2020. Ten days later, schools across the world began shutting down as the Coronavirus began sweeping the globe. I found myself taking 32 years of in-person band directing and figuring out how to be an online music educator while also going through the process of editing of this book.

While that certainly made for some interesting times, it gave me the opportunity to truly dig in and evaluate the efficacy of the very content of this book and how it would translate into whatever learning environments in which we find ourselves.

The ultimate purpose of this book is to share the protocol I created that has become the basis of the social and emotional learning needs for my students (and, truth be told, for me.) Everything I talk about in this book was true before the pandemic, and it has proven to be as powerful in a virtual environment as it is in person.

Education has been turned upside down in the wake of COVID and everything else that has come with it. More than ever, students and teachers are facing stressful situations, and that makes it difficult, if not impossible, to truly learn.

As music teachers, we are one of the few adults kids come in contact with year after year, so they will naturally turn to us and need guidance as they learn to navigate this strange new world. They are counting on us for far more than learning how play songs or learn about music history, but before we can do any of that, they need us to help them put aside the things that distract them.

Many of our students have faced traumatic situations. There is stress everywhere. And when they show up or log in for class with their minds full of those distractions and their bodies jittering with nervous energy, even the most riveting lesson can elude them.

That's where this book comes in.

I share the technique I developed years ago and have used every single day in every single class for the past three years that physically and mentally resets students (and me) by teaching them how to "tune" their brains and bodies for music class. By investing four minutes a day, my students have built the skills they need to consistently be attentive, focused, and engaged in whatever activities we are doing.

It's a very simple process and it doesn't require spending a penny.

As music teachers, we teach students how to develop all kinds of skills, from mental to physical, in order for them to be well-rounded musicians. We show them how to properly form an embouchure, the correct fingerings to use, how to read music, what proper posture looks like, and so much more.

And we always tell them to "pay attention" and "focus." But do we ever teach them *how* to pay attention and focus?

Starting with that step makes *everything* easier for them and for you. It is the foundation of solid social and emotional self-regulation that empowers the students to get out of fight-or-flight stress mode and immerse themselves in a state that allows them to be present with what you want them to be doing.

I have been teaching this process to music educators all over the world, and I am beyond excited to have finally put it in the format of a book so more teachers can benefit from what happens when you and your students "tune up" before you do anything else.

The pandemic changed a LOT of things about education. It's added more stress for everyone. Getting students focused on content will be even more challenging than it used to be.

The great news is that you can give your students the gift of learning to self-regulate, calm down, and focus without distraction through intentional design and practice. And I can help you do that!

Check out the webinar where I teach this concept by going to mPoweredEducator.com/webinars – Scroll to the Social and Emotional Learning in the Modern Music

Classroom webinar from August 6, 2020 to learn more about the program outlined in this book.

Chapter 1:

My Life's Work Is So Much More Than Just a Job

"I wrote this book because...

I had to write this book. My purpose on this planet is to be a teacher. I originally thought I was meant to be a band teacher, but I'm meant to be a teacher. Just a teacher, teaching what I learned and sharing it with those who I can serve."

This paragraph is in response to a prompt from a reflection I did in preparation for writing my first book, and it holds just as true for this book as it did when I sat down to start writing the first time.

Music education has been my whole life. I love my career. There's nothing I would change from my past. The fabulous memories, friendships, joys, trips, concerts, fundraisers, games, activities, retreats, classes, parades, and thousands of other things that happened over the years filled my life and my family's life with much to be grateful for.

But raising three kids of my own while teaching three hundred or more teenagers a day as a high school band director brought its share of challenges, too.

I saw so much change during my years as a teacher. Technology and society caused our kids to start growing up faster than they were physiologically programmed to do, and the impact on their ability to function in this world was huge.

As teachers, we find ourselves vying for our students' attention, trying to keep them engaged in class when they have constant distractions from electronic devices and all of the other stimuli to which they are constantly exposed. For the past several years, I intentionally integrated strategies in my teaching to help counterbalance the overstimulation our kids experience, and that has been a game-changer, especially now.

For the first thirty-one-and-three-quarters years of my career, there was a lot that changed, but nothing like what happened when the 2020 pandemic hit the planet and, at the speed of light, uprooted everything we ever learned about teaching. Suddenly, in what was going to be my final quarter of teaching, I found myself, along with every other teacher in the U.S. and beyond, completely reinventing how I taught as the world came to a standstill and schools were shut down across the globe. I had to learn to teach high school band online!

The first few weeks of the abrupt transition from face-to-face teaching to the isolation of being quarantined and figuring out how to meet the emotional and educational needs of my students was daunting. As we started working through what it would look like for us to continue our band classes without being together, I came to realize that the daily practices and protocols I established with my students (who often come to class with challenges like anxiety, depression, and difficulty focusing) as a way to help them focus and be present for class were even more important now. The daily practice we did in one another's presence every day – taking four minutes to do breathing and relaxation together – up-leveled our in-class experiences because of the way it synchronized all the students each day, which caused our rehearsal time to be at least three to four times more productive than in the past. I knew that since our routine had such a positive impact on our ability to bring sixty-plus teenagers together and get them focused when we were in person, it was critical that we continued to practice that same routine when we were isolated and experiencing heightened anxiety and trauma. The ritual of getting our bodies and brains to relax each day before we started class was more important now than ever.

Kids are constantly told to "sit still and be quiet," yet they're never really taught how to harness their energy and social reflexes so they can actually sit quietly and focus their attention. Guess what happens when you actually teach students how to physiologically reset their bodies and brains so all of the restless energy (side conversations, excessive physical movements, difficulty focusing, inability to pay attention or remember) gets out of their way and they are able to start with a clean slate? It's truly remarkable. It's how we are biologically programmed to function at our best, so why not work *with* nature and teach our students how to tap into this? Once you do, you will be blown away at the changes: the ease of teaching, the attentiveness of the students, the retention of content, and a million other positive changes that take place as a result of taking the time to teach students this critical skill.

Teaching kids to get into this learning state is no different than teaching them technique on an instrument. It's muscle memory – that is all. By practicing scales slowly, you train their muscles to respond in specific ways. The more you repeat patterns, the easier it is for them to execute those patterns and the quicker their responses become. The same goes for teaching kids mindfulness. Once your students practice a relaxation routine on a consistent basis, their bodies learn to be still because the muscles learn how to relax. Their brains are no longer in hyper mode; instead, they respond to this practice by learning to let go of the drama and other stuff floating around in their heads and become cleared out for whatever content or concept you want to introduce.

You have an incredible opportunity to help your students not just be successful musicians but to be exceptional human beings. Music teachers change the world. We are arguably the most influential adults on the planet. We have kids in our classes year after year after year. We watch them grow up. We are the only adults they see that frequently, sometimes even more than their parents, see them. So, we have important work to do – and we need the stamina to do it.

That's where this book comes in. If I learned about the power of teaching this skill before diving into content with my students, I could have been a healthier and more effective teacher from the start. Instead, I spent the first three decades of my career teaching the way I was taught, actively handling classroom management and correcting behaviors instead of giving my students the skills to self-regulate so I could focus on teaching. It took a lot more energy (both physically and mentally) to teach when I didn't have a daily routine to get everyone relaxed and focused.

For most of my life, I didn't know how to relax, and teaching was a hyperactivity for me. I did it well, but managing all the components of a huge music program required active work, both mentally and physically. Even teaching classes took a lot of energy. Corralling the energy of sixty kids an hour, day after day, and motivating them to meet my goals was exhausting. Once I learned the power of teaching students to relax and settle that energy down before starting to teach class, everything became so much easier for all of us.

I'm a much more effective teacher now. Instead of force-feeding kids everything I believe they should know and feel, I facilitate their abilities to tap into the music and hear the message it has for them. I learned how to help them go from states of stress – where learning is difficult, if not impossible – to a place where their brains and bodies are receptive and ready to learn, remember, and recall

15

what they're discovering. It sounds like a whole new way of teaching, but really, it's not. It's the way we were programmed to learn.

When we teach students how to get into a learning state, *teaching and learning become so much easier*, leading to less stress for you and your students.

This process can be used by children of all ages and across all socio-economic statuses, cultures, orientations, and marginalization, including over-achievers and AP/Honors kids. In fact, it's often most effective for the kids you'd least expect.

Just like a carpenter needs the proper tools *and* high-quality wood *and* a plan if he is going to create a craftsman-style piece of furniture, teachers need tools to do their jobs well, too. **One of the most powerful tools a teacher has is being able to guide their students into a readiness-to-learn state before delivering content**. This one simple step has more impact on every aspect of student growth than *any* other pedagogical tool I encountered in the more than 30,000 classes I taught over the course of my career.

This book is my way of sharing what I learned so other band directors can do the important work of teaching in a way that is easier and more effective for them and their students. I want to support them in their efforts to be positive role models and mentors for their students. I want to work with teachers who realize that our roles include shaping kids into responsible and respectful human beings through the magic of music education. It takes a lot of stamina to do this year after year, and I am here to share strategies that support dedicated music teachers who are called to change kids' lives for the better.

Under the best of circumstances, teaching is stressful and exhausting.

After our 2020 health crisis, it's going to be even more so, and unless you have a plan in place for how you'll help students cope with the strange new world in which we live, it'll be overwhelming and daunting for you and your students.

If you have a routine that already works, then now is the time to reevaluate it and see what you might need to tweak in order to meet the new needs of your students. Most of them will be affected by everything that happened as a result of the pandemic, so teaching-as-usual will be anything but usual. You know your students and community best, so you can use this book as a guide to help you assess and possibly redesign what you do in light of our new normal.

If you don't have a routine you use to help your students overcome the distractions of life so they can focus in your class, then I'm especially glad you picked up this book! Now's your chance to practice some new skills that will help you and your students get the most out of your classes in spite of the added stress, anxiety, depression, and more they'll be dealing with.

This book outlines the process I designed and implemented in my classroom and is set up to help you create a plan to successfully teach music to students who will be forever changed after this worldwide shift in education and life as we once knew it.

My work with my students always comes from a place of love. As I came to what was going to be the end of a long and fulfilling career in music education in June of 2020, I found myself being called to stay in my classroom and community a little while longer. I see the writing on the wall and know there will be massive shifts in everything we do as educators now, so I made the commitment to remain with my students and walk beside them on this journey. Providing them with the stability of our routines together during a time of upheaval and uncertainty is essential not just for them but for me, too. Now more than ever, they need to continue to practice what we were doing every day in class – relaxing amidst the chaos.

Because my students and I learned to make our classroom a place where we decompress together every day, I know I will have the stamina to be present with them as we adapt to our new ways of doing things. Even though we will all have more reasons to be distracted with each passing day and the rapid changes taking place to education and we will undoubtedly experience plenty of stressful situations, we will forge ahead with our daily routine that allows us to settle into an hour of magical music-making together, where we can put our worries and distractions on the back burner and use music as a tool to help us cope, heal, and express ourselves.

This book is the culmination of my life's work and shares the most powerful wisdom I gained from my decades of experience as a busy band-directing mom who managed to build a successful band program in spite of a million obstacles. My wish for you is that you will find it to be instrumental in helping you be that badass band director you were born to be so you can be there for your students for a long time to come.

Chapter 2:

I Love My Job but It's Killing Me

For over three decades, I have been a high school band director. I teach in the community where I serve. I teach in a large school with robust support for our music program. What started as a job where I taught three band classes and accompanied the choir in order to have a full-time contract soon morphed into a gigantic machine of a program that eventually had over three-hundred students involved in the bands, starting with *four* jazz bands at 6:30 every morning, and another *five* concert bands and *two* percussion ensembles throughout the course of the day. Then, after school, there were more rehearsals, meetings, concerts, pep band events, fundraisers, and all the other activities that came with a high school band program. It got out of hand, and it was my own fault.

I was measuring success by the numbers of students in our program, the comments we got at competitions, and the distance we traveled each spring for music festivals. While those metrics made me feel really good, they came at a cost.

As cool as it is to be in charge of a huge band program, it's physically and mentally exhausting! The three-hundred kids I teach each day deserved and needed my full attention. That in and of itself takes a lot to manage. Add the responsibilities of handling all the paperwork, email, planning, budgeting, meetings, and other things we did on a daily basis, and it's no wonder teaching was so stressful.

I truly love my job, and I put my heart and soul into it. But year after year of teaching students who were becoming more and more distracted became taxing. By the time I taught five classes filled with diverse learners armed with noisy instruments, I was overstimulated beyond belief. At the end of my instructional day, it would be really hard to regroup and take care of all the administrative duties that came along with my responsibilities. My brain was worn out from being overstimulated, and it made doing my other work so much harder.

I needed a better way to teach, or it wouldn't be feasible for me to continue in this career. It was causing me to live in a constant state of stress (which showed up as anxiety, depression, weight gain, insomnia, chronic inflammation and pain, and more) and to feel like I couldn't be an effective teacher *and* mom. For a long time, it felt like I only had the energy to be one or the other. I hadn't heard anyone else talk about balancing high school band directing and parenting, so I struggled on my own for a very long time.

I always wanted to be a high school band director. From the time I was born, I was surrounded by high school band kids and all the activities they did. My dad was the band director at the high school where my brother and sister and I went, and our family life revolved around all the band concerts, pep band events, and trips. I wanted to build a program just like that in the neighborhood where I lived and I wanted to have my own children in my program, too. As soon as I graduated from high school, I was off to Indiana University. I completed my music education degree and was ready to begin what would turn out to be an exciting, fulfilling, exhausting, and unbelievable career. I got married (right before student teaching), started my career, and started having babies. I thought I was prepared to handle it all.

Practicing my mad conducting skills at the age of 8.

My own kids are four years apart in age, and when they reached their high school years, there was a period of twelve consecutive years where one of my own children was part of the band program where I taught. I was literally living the dream I created in my mind all those years ago as I watched my dad's band program when I was a kid and imagined a time when I would be the band director and have my own children in class. What I didn't have in my dreams was a clue about what the stress and reality of being in charge of such a huge program *and* raising three children of my own would actually do to me.

In hindsight, I realize that the high school band directors I looked up to were all men. I didn't know any women who were teaching band at the high school level and who raised children. I knew plenty of successful high school band directors and plenty of successful moms, but not people who were both.

Being both a mom and band director comes with its own unique set of challenges, from having a physically demanding job *and* being pregnant at the same time to using your planning periods to pump breast milk instead of actually planning lessons and then having to plan the lessons later. Not to mention, we serve as second moms for our kids at school, carrying their emotional baggage as we worry about them after hours and in the middle of the night.

Don't get me wrong. I am not complaining, and I am not afraid of hard work. It's just that over the years and decades that I spent as a mom and band director, I didn't always have the tools I needed to do both important jobs and stay healthy. It was just too hard.

What started as a dream to build a music program that was active in the community turned into something that was too much for me to manage in the same ways I functioned when I first started teaching. Instead of enjoying the pep band events because of the joy and camaraderie they brought the band kids, I began resenting the time the events took me away from my family. It felt like everybody else's to-do lists were more important than mine, and the activities that used to be fun became chores because there seemed to be way too many of them.

For a while, I almost quit. I found myself mumbling, "I love my job, but it's killing me," as I dragged my tired body from my car to the band room through the chilly and damp winter mornings for zero period jazz band after having been at school until 10:30 the night before because of a basketball playoff game that went into overtime. I was struggling to be the mom and teacher I wanted to be. After my long workdays, my patience for my own children and husband didn't win me any Mother of the Year awards. I felt like I was failing in everything because it was so hard to keep up.

I was desperate to change things. By the time I had been teaching for twenty-five years, I was running on empty. The results of throwing myself into a job I dearly loved meant I had less and less time to do other things, like get proper sleep and eat something besides leftover mac-n-cheese or drive-thru fast food. Eventually, the lack of care I put toward staying healthy turned into me being saddled with problems that really impacted my physical and mental health and made it *so* much harder to do my job.

I could hardly focus on teaching hundreds of students each day when I was struggling with anxiety, depression, insomnia, joint pain, brain fog, and ADHD. Every task seemed to take so much effort, and every day, it was harder and harder just to keep up. It felt like it took more and more effort just to keep kids focused and on-task, and I was finding it exhausting to keep actively managing rooms full of teenagers who all had cell phones and district-issued devices to distract them from my fascinating lessons. I was really struggling to juggle it all and eventually got to the point where I was in tears in my principal's office telling him I had to quit because I just couldn't do this anymore.

I didn't end up quitting, but I did end up making some very significant changes in my work and personal lives. In order to do that, I sought help from new kinds of health care professionals because I knew the same old routine of going to the doctor, getting a new prescription to cover up whatever latest symptoms I was experiencing, and going back to work and forging ahead in spite of the struggles wasn't going to help me heal. I had to try new things in order to get different results.

After a lot of soul-searching, I realized the structure of my classes and how I operated was contributing to my poor health. The program grew so fast that I didn't always have the infrastructure in place to support it. That meant it would be me and seventy-five teenagers crowded into a space where we were practically stepping on each other, and I'd be actively managing them. That took a ton of energy – taking attendance, dealing with behaviors that sucked my attention away from the group, keeping students actively engaged even when I wasn't working with them, getting them to mark music and stay on task, cajoling them to put their phones away, organizing fundraisers, and doing all the other things that had to be done simply wore me out.

I knew if I continued operating at this breakneck pace, I wouldn't be able to serve much longer in this profession because it simply wasn't feasible. It wasn't a one-person job, but somehow, I was trying to juggle it all.

Part of my dream when I was a child envisioning being a high school band director included rehearsals where we actually spent time working on music. However, I found that, with the size of my classes and the rate at which I had to pace every lesson to keep them actively engaged, I was spending the majority of my focus actively managing their behaviors. It was hard to do hour after hour, day after day. Going straight from one class into another without getting to take any kind of break to reset, I found myself mentally worn out as I transitioned from jazz band to honors wind ensemble to a ninth-grade percussion ensemble and more. The constant shifting of from class to class and meeting the developmental stages of all my different kids adds another layer to the already-overstimulated brain of a music teacher.

What happened as I discovered how to get myself healthier literally saved my life. It helped me transform not only my physical body, but it also helped me learn strategies for dealing with symptoms of ADHD, depression, and anxiety. Over the course of about six months, and with the guidance of health care professionals, I was completely weaned off all fourteen prescriptions was on for over twenty years to manage symptoms that I no longer had!

More changes, including being nearly symptom-free from anxiety, depression, and ADHD and sleeping like a baby, began happening. Through all of this, as my health improved, I functioned so much better. It became much easier to work efficiently and get a heck of a lot more done in less time now that I was no longer struggling with so many symptoms that were exacerbated by stress.

The good news is, the things I learned that saved my own life actually taught me some important skills that I took into my classroom to create a space that intentionally reduces stress for my students and for me. I restructured how I do a lot of things. I sought out help from others. I learned how to set boundaries that allow me to serve my students and my family – and myself.

The result of my personal transformation was so profound that I couldn't help but try some of the techniques I learned with my students. I know many of them struggle with ADHD, anxiety, depression, and other chronic issues that are made worse by the way they live.

What if I could help them feel better so they could be focused on what I wanted them to be doing in class instead of being distracted by their friends, phones, and other internal and external stimuli? Knowing that they come to school with stressors that impede their ability focus and learn, what could I do to even the playing field and help all of us be more successful? How would that change my ability to teach and my students' abilities to learn?

Teaching is hard work. We don't decide to be band directors because we think it'll be easy. We don't mind hard work. In fact, we kind of thrive when we're in situations where we are multi-tasking. Lots of incredible memories are made in the late-night concerts, on trips, during pep band events, and at fundraisers. We joyfully give our time and talents to help our students experience music the way we imagine being most fulfilling. Rewriting parts, staying after school to help a kid, and being the first one in the building and last one to leave are all part of the gig, but eventually, they can dominate your life. Before you know it, you find yourself wondering how you can keep this up for much longer.

Well, you can stop wondering. This book was designed to help you get out of the rut that is weighing you down *and* set you up to continue in your music teaching career for many years to come – but without all the stress and exhaustion!

Being a badass band director isn't easy. When I was starting out in the 1980s, we didn't have the ability to connect with people who weren't in close proximity like we do today, and I didn't have any female band directors who were raising their own families who could help me figure this out, so I was in the trenches making up a lot of it as I went. There's no reason you should have to try and figure it all out on your own.

Now that I know better, I am sharing what I learned so other music teaching moms can experience the joys of both motherhood and teaching without burning out. Both teaching and motherhood offer so many rewards, and by using this book and the ideas in it as a resource, you can up-level your personal and professional lives and enjoy being a *healthy* band director and parent... without burning out.

Imagine what it would be like to have your students be attentive and responsive to your requests the first time you asked, stay engaged even when you aren't working directly with them, develop their musical skills at a faster rate, take responsibility for their own behavior and progress, and free you up to spend more time on teaching and doing the things that matter and less time re-teaching, reminding, and reprimanding students who just can't seem to get it together.

I promise you that you can get your classroom to be a place where your students work *with* you instead of you coaxing them along. You will be free to teach concepts like intonation and artistry much more effortlessly than you were, and you can do it in a way in which students respond to what you're teaching and remember it.

In the more than 30,000 classes I taught during my career (so far), I learned a thing or two about what does and doesn't work. I spent lots of time learning which processes are more effective and efficient in different situations. I attended classes and workshops, professional development and conferences, and worked tirelessly at constantly improving my craft, which is teaching. Not teaching *music* – teaching.

With an average of sixty students an hour for five hours a day, day after day, year after year, decade after decade, I developed strategies for everything: efficiently taking attendance, instructional design, assessment, classroom management, planning, teaching, communicating, fundraising, trip planning, pep band events, drum line activities, community service, inventory management, jazz festivals, budgeting, parent booster groups, and a million other things that are part of this gig. I took what I learned and created this book, which is essentially the curriculum I teach in my signature program, *Band Director Boot Camp.* I want to share what I learned so band directors like you don't have to experience all the hard lessons I went through.

This book shares the most important nuggets I distilled from everything I learned about most effectively balancing the many roles I play in the least stressful way possible. You might be surprised at the simplicity of some of the suggestions I make and doubt that something I'm saying could really accomplish what I claim. When questions come up or doubts about whether this could apply to your situation make you skeptical, be curious. Just wonder, "What if this actually worked? What would that look like for me? What would it be like for my students? What would it feel like to have time and energy for my own children?"

We teach students the way we were taught when we were students and the way we were taught to teach when we went to college. But kids today are living in a world that is causing their brains and bodies to develop in ways that they aren't biologically programmed to do, and the pedagogical tools we were trained to use aren't as effective with kids who are in constant overdrive in today's environment.

It's not up to the kids to change and adapt to our ways of teaching. It's our responsibility as adults to meet them where they are and then teach them what they need to learn. That requires having an effective strategy that *prepares them to learn* so that all the content you deliver actually gets absorbed in their brains and they can remember and use it.

The old-school way of teaching band is for the director to stand on the podium as the expert. As the director, it's up to us to be the authority on all things music. We tell the kids when they play something wrong, we tell them how to interpret a phrase, and we make sure they understand all the rules of music and replicate them so they sound just like the finest recordings. It's like teaching paint-by-numbers. We get so focused on teaching them to play the music "right" (we even go to great lengths to use rubrics and scoring guides to show them exactly what "right" looks and sounds like so they don't have to decide for themselves) that we often stifle any potential artistry they might express because they begin to see their roles as successful musicians defined as being able to reproduce exactly what was done before instead of bringing a fresh perspective.

I found over the course of my career that I became far more effective as a teacher after I progressively got more out of the way of the music. For many decades, I believed I was being the best teacher I could possibly be by going to great lengths to make sure my students were given all the answers, from what the composer intended with the work (and therefore how the students should feel about it) to the "best" parts and everything in between. I left them no opportunities to come up with their own opinions. In the system in which we're entrenched, success is measured based on how well our students played by the rules – the rules being things like artistic interpretation, phrasing, and other details of the music. I wondered if this was truly the best way to serve my students as a music teacher.

Once I got out of the way and trusted the music and my students to discover things without me being the conduit, incredible things started happening. I restructured the first four minutes of our daily routine to actually teach the students how to "tune their bodies and brains" for band. Students became more intuitive with everything, from playing in tune to how to blend in with the ensemble. Their progress began to grow at much quicker rates as they became curious about the possibilities of what they could *create* instead of just *re-create*.

What I implemented in my personal and professional lives as a result of what I learned was a game-changer for me as a teacher and a mom. As we transitioned from a pre-pandemic education time through the stressful online education and eventually to a different post-pandemic educational system that comes with a whole new set of stressors, the techniques and habits my students and

I developed will serve us well. Our four-minute mindfulness routine doesn't eliminate our stressors, but it helps us settle down and reset when we gather together, and that makes everything else easier.

The practices I describe in this book fundamentally upgraded my personal life and everything I experience in my classroom. If they didn't work, I wouldn't be traveling all over the globe teaching them, and I certainly wouldn't write books about them. I made it my mission to help other teachers find the tools they need to get back to the joy of teaching and be the real-life role models their students need.

What kind of message are we sending kids when we are frazzled, overbooked, stressed, distracted, and exhausted? They watch us and, like it or not, they see themselves in us. They reflect what they see. If we truly want to be the role model our kids need, why not be the best version of ourselves we can possibly be, especially when it makes life better for everyone we encounter?

I invite you to turn the page and begin your transformation. As Brigette Hyacinth said, "Great leadership isn't about control. It's about empowering people."

Chapter 3:

The Badass Band Director's Bible

The fact that you are reading this book indicates you are a teacher who truly cares about the students you serve. You are seeking ways in which you can continue to give them what they deserve, help them grow as humans, and give them the incredible experience of participating in a thriving music program.

This book gives you the tools you need so you have the stamina to take care of hundreds of students every day and experience a long and healthy career. I invite you to be open to new ways in which you might approach the things that are draining your energy and think about innovative ways you can explore new solutions.

How This Book Will Become Your Band Directing Bible

We all want to be exceptional music teachers, and in order to do that, we need to have systems in place that consistently and reliably work. If you are at the point where you are ready to get those systems up and running more effectively and start seeing your students flourish and your stress levels decrease, then you're in the right place.

This book was designed to be a workbook and reference in your journey as you navigate the complexities of this career. Each chapter will take you through sequential steps to help you fast-track figuring out the things that are your biggest stressors and sucking your energy and what you can do to change things.

In Chapter 9, you'll use my template to create your own "script" for the protocol you'll implement that will help you and your students go from a high-energy teacher-managed classroom to a relaxed yet engaged and student-managed classroom where music teaching (not active classroom management) becomes the new normal. *This* is the game-changer that makes *everything* you do easier while reducing the burnout that comes with the high demands of our jobs. There are various assessments and activities for you to do along the way. They're designed to help you take stock of your own practices, ideas, thoughts, dreams, goals, and more. The purpose of them is to guide you in getting clarity about what you want so you can get there in an efficient and fun way.

Since the purpose of everything in here is to help make it easier for you to do the job you love, there should be joy and satisfaction in giving yourself the gift of taking the time to do this right. It's an investment in you *and* your students *and* your family. The assessments can be done in the book, or you can use the links provided for the online version. The advantage of the online version is that you can receive feedback based on your scores without doing the math yourself!

Chapter 4 through Chapter 9 should be done in chronological order because you learn some techniques for changing habits through those chapters that will help you more effectively implement the lesson you'll put together in Chapter 9. Chapter 4 through Chapter 9 is where you will evaluate and develop how you teach in a way that is supportive to you and your students. You will

- Assess your current work/life balance through my signature Music Teacher Mojo Meter

- Identify the non-negotiables in your life (priorities, strengths, and struggles) using the Three C's: Care, Clarity, and Consistency

- Set personal and professional goals that support you as a teacher and parent as well as serving your students and community

- Use my SNaP Strategies that are designed to help you learn quick and repeatable tactics for helping yourself and your students replace bad habits with better ones and learn new skills faster and more effectively by employing techniques learned through this process

- Understand the power of the First Four Minutes and synching your students before delivering instructions, and create your own First Four Minute protocol

- Assess potential obstacles to success and have a plan for addressing those obstacles

- Have access to a multitude of resources (my webinars, podcasts, templates, and more) to support you in your teaching and personal lives

There are questions for journaling and other "homework" assignments. I urge you not to skip them because they each serve the purpose of getting you to think about things either more deeply than you normally take the time to do or to think about something from a different perspective. After all, you can't solve a problem with the same solution that hasn't been working in the past.

Observing what you already do is also an important part of your personal growth process, so start to notice the routines you and your students already have and ask yourself if they are serving the purpose you want them to serve. Just begin by noticing – and don't beat yourself up if you start to notice things that aren't optimal. Being able to recognize where you aren't meeting your own expectations is actually a sign of being ready to grow, so celebrate those opportunities and jump in with both feet.

Chapter 10 is the Coda , which includes some practical advice and a link to my website where you'll find various resources covering everything from classroom management and your personal health to getting parents to volunteer with fundraising and a whole lot more. In videos that range from four minutes to seventy-five minutes, you can dive deeper into the things that will be helpful to you in meeting your goals.

In this book, you may find ideas that cause you to think, "Sure, that may work in Lesley's school, but *my* situation is different." Please don't dismiss what I'm suggesting. I taught these skills to teachers who use them with students in Title I schools, K-12 schools, rural and inner-city schools, and schools in the suburbs. I saw the processes I am teaching in this book work with kids who struggle with things like anxiety, depression, and ADHD; who come into my classroom with distractions that include abusive homes, overbearing parents, and incredible peer pressure; who are high-achievers; who have multiple learning disabilities; boys and girls and those who are having a hard time identifying with any gender; who are marginalized and often lost in the shuffle; and who are outgoing or shy.

Now, I will continue using this same process with kids who are traumatized by the upheaval that resulted from the 2020 pandemic and resulting school closures and disrupted way of life as they once knew it.

The reason I am teaching this technique to teachers all over the world is because it works. It is based on human development and behavior and science. It's rooted in the way people learn and remember, develop behaviors, and create habits. By learning how to incorporate these concepts into your teaching routine, you will fundamentally change the way students are able to learn, and that's where the real power is. Once you help them access this learning state in your presence, you can teach them *anything!*

The great news is that you don't have to do all the research or have decades of experience as a teacher in order to tap into the benefits of this technique. What I'm about to teach you will actually become quite intuitive to you if you take the time to do the exercises and practice the techniques. Building your chops as a music teacher is just like building your chops as a musician. You must identify the habits you want to develop and practice them. That's what you'll do with your teaching – you'll refine it to the next level, practicing new and effective strategies until they become habits you don't have to intentionally focus on, and they'll keep happening anyway once you ingrain them in your muscle memory and begin working on new habits.

That's what I want to share with you: the simple and effective way I turned my classroom from being a teacher-managed place to one where the students learn the skills they need to manage their own distractions, behaviors, and learning opportunities so my focus can be on facilitating learning. With all the additional distractions they face now, it's even more critical to empower students with these self-regulating skills (for their sake and for ours!).

Stick with me as we explore ideas that are unconventional. If what you were doing isn't working for you, then

Step 1

The Moffat Music Teacher Mojo Meter

Remember how you used to do those quizzes in *Seventeen* magazine? There was so much satisfaction in checking those boxes in a series of questions that felt like they were speaking directly to you. Then, when you added up the score, you'd jump to the answer key to find the answer to your problem and what you needed to do to fix it. If you loved answering a few questions so you could immediately diagnose and solve all your problems during your awkward teenage years, then you are in luck – I have a grown-up version made just for you! Through the use of Moffat's Music Teacher Mojo Meter, you will see where your priorities, strengths, and struggles lie, and get a clear idea of what you can do to achieve your goals and do it with a healthy balance between your personal and work lives.

Take the Moffat's Music Teacher Mojo Meter assessment (https://forms.gle/68pJTBQoY3eDvsYx5). The purpose of this is for you to get an overview of where you are and where you want to be.

Don't spend a lot of time fussing over your answers. Go with the first response that comes to mind. That's the way to get the most helpful results from this assessment – the responses will be the most honest if they come from your gut. The assessment will be what you come back to time and time again in the book as you do the homework from each section. It will serve as the guide for you to achieve clarity with where you are and where you want to be.

If you skip this assessment, it will make it much harder for you to use this book and the technique I teach because you won't have a clear idea of what it is you are trying to accomplish.

It reminds me of going to the grocery store without a shopping list. You know what I'm talking about. Your cupboards are bare, so you have to go to the store, but you lack either the time or desire (or both) to plan your meals out for the week, check your fridge and pantry for items you already have on-hand that you can use, and then make a list of the items you need to get at the store. So instead, you go to the grocery store, get a cart, and begin aimlessly wandering up and down the aisles, waiting for some divine inspiration to help you magically grab all the ingredients you'll need to feed your family for the next week. But it never happens. Instead, you see things that get your attention, so you grab those items and keep pushing the cart. After a half an hour or so, you have a cart full of groceries and you're checking out.

Once you get home, you unpack the groceries and, if you're like me, inevitably stand in front of an open fridge, only to declare, "There's nothing to eat," because the random groceries you just bought don't let you create decent meals.

Do you ever notice how high the bill is when you go in without a list? When there's not a specific plan, we get distracted by what's right in front of us and we make decisions that might not serve us in the long run. We waste both time and money, whether we're talking about going to the grocery store without a list or trying to improve your music program without a clear plan of what you're working toward.

Now, think about those times when you sit down and plan your meals for an entire week. When you take the time to look at your calendar, you're able to plan meals that are easy to fix on nights when you have a pep band event or booster meeting, and if you have company coming one night, you'll likely plan a meal for a larger crowd that will take more time to make, so you'll need to write down all the extra ingredients to make sure you aren't caught unprepared.

When you take the time to invest in assessing what you are trying to do, whether it's going shopping for a week's worth of groceries or making and executing a plan for getting your band to perform at Carnegie Hall, then you can begin the process of deciding what steps you'll take need to get there and what tools you'll need to get you there

If you've created a shopping list based on meals you've planned, you end up getting your shopping done more efficiently and with much less frustration than when you show up at the store without a list, your bill isn't likely to be as out-of-control, and you'll have the things on hand that you need throughout the week to make all the meals you and your family need. Taking the time to clarify your goals (specific meals on specific days based on afternoon and evening activities) helped you plan how to reach them (write a shopping list, get those items) and you were able to do it quickly and effectively.

This assessment is like making your shopping list. It will help you identify what you are trying to accomplish so you'll know what the logical next step is to move you closer to those goals.

This is how you build the roadmap for how you'll teach in a post-pandemic educational system, so be honest and be ready to find out just how possible it is to create an atmosphere of collaboration and easy-to-manage classes in spite of the trauma and extra challenges you and your students may experience. Once you have a clear vision and a roadmap, the rest of the pieces fall into place much easier.

After you finish Moffat's Music Teacher Mojo Meter, grab a journal or use some other device where you write down important things. At the top of the paper, write the date it will be *one year from today*. And then, as if it is actually that day, write your response to these three prompts as if what you are writing about already happened. Don't worry about *how* these things will happen, just write them as if they already have happened:

1. This year, the best thing to happen professionally was...

2. This year, the best thing to happen in my personal life was...

3. This year, I am most proud of...

These statements will be powerful because they serve as a place for you to aim your focus. Come back to them when you feel overwhelmed or are having difficulties making decisions as they will serve to get you back on-track as you are reminded of your dreams and goals.

I remember August 12, 2018, writing in my brand-new journal, "#1 NY Times best seller: mPowered Educator: Mindfulness, Meals, Music, and Movement." I had no idea what I meant by all that. I was thinking about writing a book, but I hadn't told a soul or even spoken the words out loud until the day I wrote these words in my journal. It was the first day I articulated and admitted to myself how much I wanted to reach that goal.

8/12/18

POWER

M Powered
Mindfulness, Meals, Meditation, Music
Mantras,

#1 NYTIMES 2018
BESTSELLER

From my head to my journal to done!

I had no idea what to do next, so I found someone who successfully wrote bestselling books and taught other people how to do it and hired her. She's an expert at helping people reach their goals of writing a book, and ninety days later, my first book was done! We uploaded the eBook to Amazon and the Kindle version became an international best seller in three categories in December of 2018. Talk about lightning fast!

The reason I was able to reach this goal so quickly and with such ease is because I claimed my goal with clarity. I used words that clearly identified what I intended to do, and I literally pictured myself being a successful author.

46

Once I knew exactly what I wanted to do, the next step was to find resources to help me get there. If I hadn't been clear with my goals, I wouldn't have known where I was going or what resources I needed to help me get there. I would have remained stuck with the idea of writing a bestselling book in my head instead of actually writing two books in a year and a half.

Let me repeat what I said a moment ago when sharing the contents of my journal: *I had no idea what I really meant by what I wrote.* I simply put down what was in my head and heart. Within three months, I wrote a book that outlined my mPower Method, which uses a mindful approach to using music, meals, and movement to empower women to be healthy and happy. The very words I jotted into my journal manifested into reality once I was clear about what I wanted to do. The process of journaling is incredibly powerful for expediting progress toward any goal, so harness the power of consolidating your thoughts in one place and let them simmer together.

One year to the day after I wrote these words in my journal, I received notification that the publisher shipped the print books. Once I claimed my goal, I was able to seek the resources I needed to reach (actually, *exceed* would be a more accurate term) the very goals that started as dreams.

This is why you are doing this exercise. You will come back to your answers from the MTMM and these prompts as you go through the book. They will serve to help you stay on-track and moving toward your goals when it can otherwise be tempting to get distracted.

So, take a deep breath, spend a moment thinking about your students and why you do what you do, and then answer these questions from your heart. Honest reflection is the first step in moving toward your next achievements! https://forms.gle/68pJTBQoY3eDvsYx5

Scoring Rubric:

15 questions worth 1 to 5 points each (total max possible = 75)

If you scored between 15 and 40 points, then it's likely there are significant stressors in several areas that may make teaching extra challenging for you now. The good news is that if you go through all the exercises in this book and do the work, you will be able to use the tools you learn to help you and your students learn to reduce external stressors and focus on teaching and learning. No matter how adept you are at presenting content, if you are having difficulties getting students who are distracted, traumatized, anxious, and depressed to pay attention to what you are teaching, they won't be able to learn what you're teaching. Trust the process, do the work, and watch what happens!

If you scored between 41 and 59 points, you are probably in a place that is more stressful than you'd like it to be, but you are managing pretty well in most areas of your life. You will benefit from the exercises in this book as

48

they will help you fast-track identifying and changing the habits that aren't serving you or your students into ones that transform the way students respond to you and your teaching. As you work through the book, you'll likely be ready to try implementing small changes with yourself and your students so you can test them out before making major changes. When you do that, be sure to notice what happens as you intentionally help students learn how to learn.

If you scored between 60 and 75, you are probably in pretty good shape for dealing with most of the challenges that come in today's classrooms with students who are experiencing overstimulation, lots of anxiety, high rates of depression, and trauma. This book can serve to provide you additional tools and strategies that will likely seamlessly complement what you are already doing in your classroom.

Chapter 5:

Step 2

Identifying the 3 C's: Care, Clarity, and Consistency

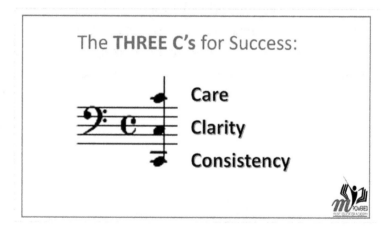

The **THREE C's** for Success:

Care

Clarity

Consistency

Music teachers are perhaps the most influential adults on the planet. I know that sounds crazy but hear me out.

During a child's first eighteen years of life, there are many people who will have an impact on him, from parents and other family members to teachers and friends and everyone else with whom he comes into contact. Kids will have most of their teachers for one year. They may be involved in sports and have coaches for multiple years, but generally, that's only for a season at a time. They spend more time at school than they do at home in many cases, and when they're at school day after day and year after year, the teacher they have most consistently, the one adult (other than their parents) who sees them on a daily basis as they grow over the course of several years, the person who notices the subtle changes in their personalities and does so much more than just teach them content, is their music teacher.

Elementary music teachers have kiddos from the time they're in kindergarten until fifth or sixth grade. Middle school music teachers (God bless these special folks!) have their students during those important formative (albeit awkward) years and have the additional joy of escorting kids through puberty and all the fun that goes with that stage of life. High school directors have all the time we spend with kids in class plus all the extra field trips, performances, festivals, games, retreats, trips, fundraisers, dances, and other activities that give us the opportunities to get to know the kids way beyond what most teachers get to do.

To top it all off, not only do music teachers have students for many years in a row, we also have large groups of students, so we are able to impact hundreds of students every year. How cool is that?

It's also a lot of responsibility! As the adults who have the experience of sharing so much time and energy with our students and getting to shape them into the adults they will become, we want to do our best to help them in every way possible.

In order for you to do your job the way you want to do it, you'll want to protect yourself from getting distracted by things that take you away from helping students, so we are going to use the Three C's of Success as a filter for how you determine where to spend the bulk of your time.

Using my ideas and your responses to Moffat's Music Teacher Mojo Meter and the other homework in here, you will be able to identify your biggest barriers to achieving your goals and the simplest strategies to solving it.

Now that you completed Moffat's Music Teacher Mojo Meter, you have a starting point for looking at where you were, where you are, and where you want to go. You can refer to it when you need to remember why you started reading this book in the first place. It will remind you of how you were feeling when you decided it was time to take the next step in your career and help keep you on track as you move through this book and your school year.

The First C: CARE

It's time to take stock of the things you really care about, the things that *truly* have an impact. There are a lot of ways to look at "care." I'd like to talk about it in the context of *caring about who you serve and what you do.*

There were two questions in the MMTMM that asked you about caring. What was your response to these statements?

- I love my job.
- I know what I am doing makes a difference in kids' lives.

Ultimately, if you don't agree or strongly agree with these two statements (at least 85 percent of the time), then this job is nearly impossible to do. It is simply too difficult to put forth the effort and energy required to truly make a difference in kids' lives and to do all the extra stuff you have to do outside of your contracted workday if you don't feel it's worth it.

There are sacrifices to be made when it comes to building a music program, that's for sure, but when things we do as a teacher are seen as a "sacrifice" instead of an opportunity to serve, then that's when we begin to feel off balance.

When I first started teaching, I loved the part of my job that involved after-school and evening activities. It was during those events that I had a chance to have informal conversations with kids and get to know them better. We had so much fun and it really was joyful. Then, one game a week became two or three games a week, plus the regular concerts and festivals. I still had zero period jazz band every day, and by the age of 32, I was raising three of my own kids, I played piano at church every Sunday, I was on various committees, I ran our booster program, I was planning huge spring trips, and the list goes on and on.

By the time I was in my second decade of teaching, the bonding and teambuilding that used to happen organically during our extra band activities got lost as we got so busy that it became more about getting through each event than being there to serve my students. That's when I had to step back and reevaluate whether or not I was truly serving my students and their needs by overscheduling them with activity after activity.

My speaking coach, Majeed, helped me get some perspective on this when he said, "Work is love in action." That really put it all in perspective for me. I care about my students and the people they become. My work is my way of helping them develop into amazing human beings through the magic of music education. I truly loved doing what I do, and after reevaluating each component of our music program, I pared it back to the activities that supported the kind of life lessons I wanted to teach my students (you know – a love of music, collaboration, commitment, friendship, pride in excellence, teamwork, goal setting, and how to be awesome humans). At first there was resistance, of course, because it meant restructuring things in new ways and some people felt like things were being taken away from them. But, when I took the time to thoughtfully consider my priorities and listen to the stakeholders (students and administrators) about what was important to them, I was able to find the balance necessary to allow me to serve my students, school, and community while no longer neglecting my family and personal life. But none of that could have happened until I could articulate with clarity exactly what my goals were.

I had to know in my heart of hearts that the activities and other things I was doing with and for my students were serving their intended purpose and not distracting the kids or me from our primary focus – and once I had a clear vision of what the music program should offer for students, it became much easier to make decisions to support the things we deemed important and let go of the activities that were no longer of service to our musicians. Sometimes that was very hard to do because of expectations of the community (imagine the response when you cut back on having your band at sporting events several times a week ... and then imagine how much better your students could function during their classes if they weren't so exhausted from going to school all day, going to a job after school, playing in pep band for basketball games at night, and then having to do all their homework late into the night). Once you start evaluating what's important for you and your students, you'll find decisions easier to make and progress toward your goals to be much more rapid.

Here's your homework: Look at the questions below. Take a few minutes to really think about your honest answers and then use a journal or your computer to respond. These questions are designed to help you refocus on what your core values are. Coming back to those core values as you reevaluate your current situation and what you'd like to create in the future will make the process much easier. It helps you align your purpose and passion while giving you a process to support you in achieving your goals.

Before you answer the questions, take a few minutes to **reflect on why you became a music teacher.** I suggest reading through these questions and then listening to a piece of music that puts you in a frame of mind where you feel good. Let the music flow through you and then see what is revealed. For me, I put on the song "From Now On" from *The Greatest Showman*. The lyrics in that piece remind me that when all the distractions start to pile up (fancy band trips, extra pep band events, more fundraisers, lots of extra performances, testing, festivals and competitions, etc.), it's essential to remember what's *really* important. After the 2020 school shutdowns, it really put into perspective for me that my intentional focus on what was going on *in* my classroom, where every student gets to participate, is the most critical part of what I do. If I made trips and festivals our focus, then in the spring of 2020, when every festival, trip, concert, and gathering was cancelled, my students and I would have felt an even greater loss. As Hugh Grant's character sings over and over in this song, "And we will come back home, home again." This reminds me that my band room is the home where I nurtured thousands of teenagers over the years. As long as I don't get distracted with everything else that goes along with it, I can serve these incredible kiddos who are part of our amazing band family.

Now it's time for you to reflect on why you do what you do and what your priorities are. There are no right or wrong answers, but the more you can articulate your responses to these questions, the easier it will be for you to make progress and reach your goals.

So, find your song, let the music sweep over you, and then grab a pen or sit down at your computer and answer these questions from the bottom of your heart.

1. Do you love your job, or at least most aspects of it?

2. What do you love most about it?

3. What is the most challenging part of your job?

4. Who was your biggest influence in becoming a music teacher?

5. What did that person do that made such an impact on you?

6. Why did you want to become a music teacher?

7. How do you want students to feel in your presence?

8. What do you want students to remember about you?

9. What do you think they'll remember?

10. What else do you care about in your life?

The Second C: CLARITY

My husband and I were in Washington, D.C., last summer and woke up early on a sunny Sunday morning. We headed to the Potomac River and decided it would be fun to rent a kayak. We'd never done that before, so it seemed like getting a double kayak was the best idea. (My theory was that if I got tired of paddling, he could get us back to shore!)

We went into the little shack by the side of the river, rented a kayak, put on our bright orange life vests, and hopped in our two-person kayak. As a type-A control freak, I gave my husband the DL on what we were going to do. I said we were going to paddle to the area under the bridge, which was about a half mile up the river, so we could get out and explore for a little while before making our way back to the dock.

Since this was the first time either of us had been in a kayak, we didn't know what to expect. I was surprised to find out it was a lot harder than it looked. I was a little embarrassed at the fact that people who looked to be a good ten to twenty years older than us were passing us, but I rationalized that they must be more experienced. When I saw even more people going faster than we were, I figured there must be an undercurrent where we were that was making it difficult for us to gain any momentum.

Then I turned around and confirmed our destination with my husband. I said, "We're going over to the area under the bridge, correct?" But this time when I asked the question, I also pointed ... to the *left* side of the bridge. That's when my husband said, "Yes, but I was heading to the *right* side of the bridge." We just spent the past thirty minutes literally paddling against each other without realizing it!

I had a goal. I knew what it was. My husband had a goal. He knew what it was.

Our inability to reach that goal came from the simple fact that we lacked *clarity* in communicating exactly what the desired outcome was, so we unintentionally got in each other's way and progress toward *both* of our goals was impeded. As soon as we got clear on *exactly* where we were headed, we were able to quadruple our progress because our efforts were going toward the same outcome.

Setting goals reminds me of the story I told about grocery shopping. When I take a half an hour and sit down with my calendar and Pinterest, I can easily plan meals for my family for the week. I simply need to look at all the activities we have going on, find meals that are healthy and doable based on how much time we have available to spend cooking each night, make a list of ingredients I need to get at the store, double-check my fridge and pantry to make sure I've thought of everything, and I'm good to go.

Think about the last rehearsal you had that didn't go as planned. Did things not go well because 1) you really didn't have a clear outcome in your own mind that you communicated with the students ahead of time, or 2) you or the students truly couldn't accomplish the task?

If your answer is number 2, then that's an easy fix. You just need to break down the task into simpler steps and teach it in smaller chunks or in different sequencing.

If you answered number 1, there's also an easy fix, but it's one people tend to be resistant to try because they don't see the purpose or don't want to "waste time" with this step. Let me caution you that *skipping this step of starting with a desired outcome will cause you to lose countless hours of productive rehearsal time (and sleep) reteaching and redoing things that you could have done easily if you were clear with your objective in the first place.*

If you find yourself "wasting rehearsal time" on a regular basis, ask yourself if you a) told your students the songs you are playing, or 2) told them what you want them to know and be able to do as the result of your work on that song? For example, do you ask students to play a part over and over hoping it will get better, or do you tell them, "Our goal is to play from letter A to letter B at 120 beats per minute with 90% accuracy or better. We will start at 96 beats per minute and gradually move the metronome as we master each new tempo." If you take ten seconds and articulate the common goal, you'll find it to be much easier for you and your students to accomplish what you set out to do.

Getting clarity with your goals is key to achieving them and learning to do this for yourself and with your students will save you much time and wasted efforts.

My husband and I could have easily accomplished the task of kayaking a half a mile in far less time than it took us on that sunny summer Sunday morning, but we weren't successful because of the lack of clarity in communicating with one another. How often does that happen in your classroom? Do you ever wonder why kids aren't progressing the way you want them to? Do they know what you want them to do?

Clarity is vital. When we know *what* we want, then we can start to work on *how* we'll get it. Often, it's the process of defining exactly what we want that is harder than reaching the goal itself. The most important thing to remember is that a compass will show you every direction – the trick is knowing where you want to go so it can point you in the direction you need to go to get there.

The Third C: CONSISTENCY

We've all heard the phrase, "How you do one thing is how you do everything." Yup. 100 percent true. The real difference between being successful or not successful in *anything* is the consistency with which you show up.

Have you ever gone to a fantastic conference session and learned something totally awesome that you just *knew* was going to change how your classroom ran, and you couldn't wait to show up on Monday morning and do that new activity? Remember how exciting it was to think about the promise of having a fun and new way to engage your kids? And remember how great it was... until it wasn't? The novelty wore off, the kids showed resistance, or you got too busy to practice this new technique on a regular basis. It ended up being just another thing you tried that failed.

Did "it" fail, or did the way you implement it fail?

Consistency is required to achieve anything. That's true whether we are talking about achieving success or achieving failure.

Think about the kid who's totally amazing at playing video games. It's because he consistently practices (though his mother probably calls it "wasting time") the skills he needs to develop to master the games. Likewise, a student who consistently gets away with disruptive behavior continues to improve his skill at being disruptive because he's practicing that skill.

We literally program ourselves and our students to do what we repeatedly do. If we consistently bounce from one classroom management technique to another in an effort to find ways to control our classrooms, students will learn that we are not dependable with our expectations, so they will consistently miss the moving targets. But if we teach with intentionality and are consistent with practicing the new habits we want our students to learn, we will more effectively guide them to develop skills that will help them become better musicians, and in the process they will also learn all those other life-lessons that come with a quality music education, like teamwork, collaboration, artistry, and grit.

The most successful parents and teachers know that it's the consistency with the "little things" (which really are the big things) that make all the difference in how a child develops. That starts with consistent expectations (students and parents need targets and boundaries so they know what they're working toward) for everything from behaviors and participating in class to fully showing up and being the dependable adult they need as a role model.

Even on the hard days. Especially on the hard days.

Kids look to us for so much more than just teaching them how to play songs. They *want* to become amazing adults. They want our help (even when they act like they don't.) They need our guidance. Most of all, they need us to *care* about them, be *clear* with what we want them to do and why we want them to do it, and be *consistent* and dependable so they can rely on our guidance through not just their music journey, but their life journey.

I'm going to ask you to reflect on something that didn't work for you. Try to think of a real example, and then honestly respond to each of these questions for that situation.

- ♪ What is an example of something you tried to do in your class that you thought was going to be the best thing ever, but it failed?

- ♪ Why do you think it failed?

- ♪ What was the outcome?

- ♪ What would you have liked the outcome to be instead?

- ♪ Give an example of a time when you were successful with implementing something in your classroom or personal life, even when you met with resistance or it got hard to do.

- ♪ What did you do when you faced the resistance?

- ♪ What helped you be consistent when it would have been easier to quit?

- ♪ Why was it important to consistently teach this concept?

♪ What were the results of consistent implementation of your new technique?

♪ Do you tend to be consistent with routines, expectations, and things that are important to you or do you give up and question yourself when a student, parent, administrator, or your cat shows the least bit of resistance?

What does this all mean?

Music teachers are usually in this gig for the long-haul. Most of us don't want "quick fixes" to whatever we're trying to solve. We actually want to help our students build a strong foundation in everything, from their musical skills and their personal development to rehearsal etiquette and community engagement. But it's often hard to justify taking the time to do the things it takes on a daily basis to help students develop into the musicians and humans we want them to be... unless we are *clear* about why we *care* about what we are doing, and we *consistently* take the actions needed to support them on their journeys.

In the daily grind and when pressures are real (upcoming concert, basketball game, testing, etc.), consistency can feel impossible. But when we lack consistency, we tend to settle for a short-term solution (think writing in positions for a trombone player instead of teaching him to read note names), and that doesn't serve our students in the long-term. It might seem like it does because in the short-term, students might accomplish the goal of playing a specific song. But, they sure won't build the skills they need in order to learn new music. In the long run, taking the time to build the skill properly in the first place will save hours of wasted time down the road.

I remember resorting to a short-term solution with my hair one time. My roots were beyond overgrown. The grey streak down the part-line of my hair made me look like Cruella de Vil, but I just didn't have time to go to the salon and get my roots colored, so I stopped by the drug store on the way home from school and picked up a can of root cover-up spray. Seemed like a great idea – and what an ingenious time-saver this invention was! Instead of sitting in the salon for three hours while I had my hair professionally colored, all I had to do was spray the dark brown hair dye onto my roots and they'd magically disappear. Problem solved.

Except I live in Seattle, where it rains. A lot. And rain is wet. Hair dye that is sprayed on top of your hair instead of being soaked up by the hair shaft doesn't exactly stay put in a downpour. In less than three minutes, my grey roots were once again visible, and that dark brown hair dye was making its way down my face in vertical streaks as the rain washed the color right out of my hair and down my cheeks. Super attractive.

My point is that taking shortcuts when we are in a hurry usually backfires. I no longer see the value in buying the temporary brown hair dye spray, using it on my hair, running the risk of being caught in the rain and having it run down my face, and having it rub off all over my pillowcase and towels when I sleep. It became worth it to me to avoid looking cheesy and using this shortcut because I found that I felt better about how I looked and liked not having to worry about silly things like wet hair dye residue on my face when I just avoided the extra-long root growth in the first place.

I now consistently set up my next hair appointment as I'm leaving the salon. I make time for it in my calendar and I tell myself I'm looking forward to it, even if I think I'm too busy to go. Then, I show up. Since I've been doing that consistently now for quite some time, I haven't run the risk of being a fashion disaster due to a face full of hair dye streaks! I found that the practice of consistently taking care of my personal needs is actually quite nice, so there's that bonus, too.

Now that you have an idea of the core principals of being successful as a badass band director – the Three C's: Care, Clarity, and Consistency – let's move on and apply them to your top personal and professional goals in Chapter 6.

Step 3

Identifying Your Priorities

In this chapter, you are going to identify the priorities you have in your personal and professional lives. You've probably done an exercise like this before but tossed those goals aside when life got in the way of accomplishing them. This time when you go through this process, remind yourself that this is an essential step in making your path to success as straight as possible.

If you don't know *what* you're trying to accomplish, you won't know what to do to accomplish it, and everyone will end up frustrated. The same thing holds true for your personal and professional goals. If you don't take the time to clearly identify what you *want* to do, then how in the world will you know what you *need* to do to succeed? Investing the time and effort into clarifying your goals and articulating them in writing is going to pay off by saving you months or years of progress made in baby steps as opposed to the giant leaps you can take when you clearly see your target.

We all heard about SMART goals (Specific, Measurable, Achievable, Relevant, Time-bound) and probably rolled our eyes during staff meetings as someone droned on and on about the importance of setting goals that had these attributes. It often seems like it's wasting time and effort to take the time to do all this goal setting when we have lessons to plan and concerts to prepare for, so we often take a short cut and skip this and then wonder why we are in a rut or so stressed out that we don't know how to get off the I-feel-like-my-hair's-on-fire rollercoaster.

It was when I finally had the courage to articulate my own personal and professional goals *in writing* and share them with people who could support me in achieving them that I finally saw myself rapidly moving toward (and surpassing!) the goals of which I had previously only dreamed.

As you get ready to write down your personal and professional goals, take the opportunity to really listen to your heart. Remind yourself why you wanted to be a band director in the first place. What did you want your students to know, do, and feel because they were in your class? Does that still drive you? Connecting with the emotion behind the reason will help you be in alignment with your priorities so you are serving the purpose you intended to serve.

There is power in claiming what you intend to do. Once you put it out there ("out there" might actually be in your journal or notebook), you convey your thoughts into something concrete. When ideas go out of your head and onto paper, they begin the transformation process and can then continue the momentum.

As you do the homework at the end of this chapter, don't worry about how you'll achieve your goals. That's really not relevant at this point. The purpose of setting goals is to *dream* about the possibilities. Figuring out how to reach them happens later, so don't get bogged down in the details right now.

I shared several stories about goal setting already (kayaking, grocery shopping) to illustrate that we first need to understand our desires so we can figure out how we want to reach them.

The first step in achieving a goal is to actually have a goal! We get so wrapped up in *how* we'll achieve our goals that sometimes we don't even let ourselves dream in the first place. So, for this exercise, I want you to abandon the "safe" way to do things and really dream. Remember when you were a kid and you imagined being an astronaut, superhero, or a ballerina? You didn't interrupt yourself with the practical reasons concerning why those lofty career goals might not be possible. Instead, you used your pillowcase as a cape and put on your mom's lipstick and declared yourself to be Wonder Woman. You just were. You acted like her and felt like her. You believed you *were* her as you stood in the living room with your hands on your hips and head held high as you prepared to take over the world.

I want you to bring that same joy and belief into this exercise. That's what I did nearly two decades ago when I got an outlandish idea and set a goal to achieve something I didn't have a clue how to make happen.

It was in January of 2002 when my husband and I flew to New York City to see one of my students, JJ, perform at Carnegie Hall. He was accepted into a national honor orchestra and I wasn't about to miss this once-in-a-lifetime experience of witnessing one of my students playing in one of the most prestigious halls in the world!

Wearing our Sunday best and beaming with pride as we entered the concert hall, I remember sitting in the red velvet chairs, looking up at the magnificent stage and feeling all the feels as I squeezed my husband's arm and said, "How many teachers can say they've had a student perform at Carnegie Hall?" It was a remarkable experience that is forever etched in my memory as I watched JJ walk on that stage with tears streaming down my face. That was such a joyful experience that I encouraged other students to audition for this select annual ensemble experience, and couple of years later, I returned to New York with *three* other students to watch them have the same honor of performing on that infamous stage.

But the story doesn't end there. I had a crazier dream. I was sure it was off-the-charts out-of-reach, so I didn't tell anyone, except my husband George, about it. I thought that since it was so cool to have four students perform at Carnegie Hall, it would be even cooler to have a whole band perform there! I knew the likelihood of giving a concert at that venue with a high school band was pretty slim, but I became curious about the possibility.

In the spring of 2007, I recorded Honors Wind Ensemble's performance at our regional large group festival. Without telling the students, I sent the recording to the producers for a company that books Carnegie Hall concerts. I waited, and waited, and waited.

Then, on the first Saturday morning of spring break, I woke up early and checked my email. There, in the reading pane, one of the subject lines was, "Jackson Band's Audition Results for Carnegie Hall." My tummy flipped. I was shaking. Did I dare open it?

I said a prayer and clicked the email to read the message, and when I saw the first line saying, "We'd like to congratulate the Jackson High School Honors Wind Ensemble on your upcoming performance at Carnegie Hall," I couldn't believe it! This crazy dream I had just became real... and I had to wait *ten more days* before I could share the news with my students!

Needless to say, I immediately woke my husband up (it was 5:30 a.m. on a Saturday – I figured he wouldn't mind). For the next ten days, I went from being super stoked to being scared to death. Suddenly, I wondered what the heck I got myself into. Just because we played a few pieces of music really well for our regional festival didn't necessarily mean we were worthy of this prestigious stage, did it? Who was I to conduct on the same stage where Tchaikovsky, Bernstein, The Beatles, and other legends performed? How would I convince the entire group (and their parents) to raise nearly a quarter of a million dollars to make this dream a reality?

Clearly, I was in over my head. Or was I?

That was the longest spring break ever. I am probably the only teacher who was ever that excited to go back to school after break. I could not wait to share the news with my students, especially because they didn't even know this was something I thought about. They were going to be shocked.

Monday morning finally came, and I will never forget trying to suppress a grin as I told my students that I had an email I needed to share. The looks on their faces were priceless as they began processing what I was telling them. I saw how excited they were to do this, and together, we decided to pursue this dream now that the opportunity availed itself.

The dream (goal) was no longer just mine. Once I articulated it to my students and their parents and then to administrators and the school board, we had a team of people behind us, helping us raise money and take all of the other necessary steps to pull off a trip and performance of this magnitude. There was a lot of work involved, but when we all knew the results would be the opportunity to perform at Carnegie Hall, it became doable when we all were working toward the same goal. What once seemed like insurmountable goals – playing at a venue like this, raising this kind of money, and being able to include nearly every kid in the ensemble in a trip 3,000 miles from home – became doable when we knew what we wanted to do and we all agreed to do it. On Memorial Day weekend in 2008, I shared the stage at Carnegie Hall with sixty-seven high school students who had banded together to achieve what most musicians only dream of doing. And in the process of preparing for that event, the entire music program in our school up-leveled as we became the kind of music department that was worthy of performing at venues of this caliber.

That's why it's important for you to take the time to clearly articulate your goals. Just thinking about them isn't enough to get that spark that's required to set them on fire so you can manifest them faster and more easily. You must make a commitment to what you want to do, or you'll be stuck, your students will be stuck, and you'll feel like you're expending all kinds of time and energy without anything to show for it.

We need to have the courage to name our goals. You don't fail if you don't meet your goals; you fail to meet your goals when you don't have any goals. If you don't reach a goal, at least you knew where you were trying to go, what you did that worked to get you to move toward the goal, and what you did that got in your way of achieving your goal. Then, you are empowered to take new action. Nothing was wasted because you learned something in the process.

Once I decided I wanted to take my students to perform at Carnegie Hall, I began taking the steps needed to get them there, even though it seemed really out of reach. It started with making sure they had the musical chops to play a concert like that, so my planning and rehearsals became a little more intentional and focused, and the kids began making faster progress. By the time we went to the regional festival in March of 2007, they were playing better than they ever had before, and our performance at that festival represented the new level we were reaching. Because of the growth the students made since I had this goal in mind, I found myself looking at an email inviting us to New York City to give a concert on Memorial Day weekend of the following year.

Now, it's your turn to *dream big*. For this homework assignment, I want you to think about what you want to achieve in your personal and professional lives in the short term (one year) and long term (five years). But *before you start this assignment*, take a little time to really be present with your ideas. Set aside an hour. Before you make your lists – which can be bullet points, sentences, or whatever format helps you convey your goals to yourself in a way that is helpful for you – take the time to get your head in the right place. Remember the story about going to the grocery store without a list? Don't try to shortcut things by skipping this step of cultivating and writing down your goals. The investment of time is miniscule compared to the amount of time (and pain and agony and money) you'll save in the long run.

Wherever you are journaling or writing your goals, write the date *one year* from today on the top of the page. Then write down all the things you really want to happen in your professional life and in your personal life as if they already happened. When I wrote "#1 NY Times best seller

2018" in my journal, it was as if I was simply stating a fact that already happened.... Sure enough, just a few months later, I wrote a book that hit #1 best seller status as a Kindle book. Not exactly a New York Times best seller, but not too shabby for a first-time author!

Writing our goals down is another way of visualizing our success before it happens. Perhaps you've had your students visualize a performance while you talk them through the logistics. Maybe you told a story about a piece of music so students could imagine it and have a concept in their minds as they played it the first time. These are techniques we use to train their brains to practice a skill without actually going through the motions. You can use this same technique on yourself by writing your goals as if they were already achieved. It's simply a more formal version of visualization.

Your homework for this chapter is to identify what you want and why you want it. If you don't know what you want your students to know and be able to do, then how will you know what to teach them? Identifying the *what* is Step #1. (This is Clarity, from the Three C's in the previous chapter.) Having a *why* behind them that motivates you to keep going when it gets challenging is the most effective way for overcoming obstacles that will arise and tempt you to give up or take shortcuts. (This is identifying what you Care about from the Three C's.)

For me, taking my students to perform at Carnegie Hall was a goal, but the *reason* (the *why*) behind the goals was that I wanted my students to know what it was like to achieve the impossible! I knew setting a goal that was so high would also serve as a catalyst for up-leveling the program as a whole. I was right. We didn't just do a Carnegie Hall performance then loosen the reins and slip back into old habits. Instead, we built up new skills as we became the kind of band and music program worthy of performing on that stage. We embodied the characteristics of conductors and musicians who performed before us on that stage, studying scores and practicing a little more as well as stepping up as leaders within our program. The ripple effect was incredible. That one collective goal changed the trajectory of our music program, and now, whether we are on that prestigious stage or in the high school gym performing for an assembly, we bring that same level of excellence to all we do because it became our new norm as we worked toward this common goal.

On May 23, 2020, I was scheduled to conduct my fourth concert with my band at Carnegie Hall. What started as a crazy dream was about to become a reality for the 97 people who had done the hard work to prepare to go to New York for their once-in-a-lifetime experience. Then, plans for the trip came to an abrupt halt as we said good-bye to our students on March 13 and schools closed for the remainder of the year because of the pandemic.

Delivering the devastating news to my students and their parents via a webinar just a few weeks later after it became evident that the trip we planned for a year was no longer viable was so hard to do. What I learned from this process is that while the goal of performing at Carnegie Hall was the driving force behind the motivation for some of the students to work as hard as they did, through that hard work, our daily classroom experiences became phenomenal. In our attempts to become an ensemble worthy of performing on that stage, we up-leveled everything we did in class and as individuals to ensure our end-product would be exceptional. That process gave us music and memories that brought us joy, laughter, goosebumps, tears, and all kinds of other emotions that come from the camaraderie that takes place in a music room where everyone has a collective vision.

Losing the opportunity to take our music to the Carnegie Hall stage was a tough pill to swallow, but ultimately, our program, the students' in-class experiences, and the growth we all made as we pushed ourselves to become the best musicians we could be will remain long after May 23 comes and goes.

What I'm trying to say is that you may or may not reach your goals in the way you imagine. I didn't get to conduct at Carnegie Hall on May 23, 2020, but I did get to help my students become better musicians, collaborators, and artists in the process of preparing for a performance of that caliber. That's still a win.

So, now, you get to dream. Read through the homework below and then give yourself the gift of doing it. Don't be afraid to feel excited and remember what it felt like when you first envisioned being a band director. Your goal is to be able to be the band director you dreamed of being without the stress and exhaustion that comes with it burning you out. Let this process help you get there faster than if you just kept plugging away at the same pace you were going. Bringing your awareness back to your goals will help keep you from getting distracted by the activities that can otherwise overtake a busy band director's life. This exercise gives you a way to brainstorm ideas and then narrow down where you should start to transform your music program into one that's in line with your vision and sustainable for both you and your students.

Homework Alert

Grab your journal and let your imagination run wild.

1. Pop in your headphones and listen to a song or meditation that puts your mind in a place where you are not distracted by other thoughts, to-do lists, or noises. Pick a piece of music that puts you in a positive state of mind.

2. Set a timer for 15 minutes and respond to whatever comes to mind for these prompts:
   a. How do I want my students to feel in my presence?
   b. What do I want my students to be able to do as a result of being in my classes?
   c. What makes me happy?
   d. How do I want to feel in one year?
   e. What do I want for my students?
   f. What do I want for myself?

Then, set a timer for fifteen minutes and write whatever comes to mind.

Don't judge; just write until you can't think of another idea. Then, go through and combine ideas that are similar and make a more user-friendly list that has your one- and five-year goals.

Once you identify what your goals are, you must honestly answer the question as to *why* you want to achieve them.

After you make your big brainstormed lists, look them over, pick your top two or three personal and professional goals, and make a commitment to them. By journaling out your answers to these prompts, you're well on your way to making your dreams come true!

♪ *What* are your top two or three goals for your personal and professional life in the next year? The next five years?
  □ For example, "My students will participate in a jazz festival next year," or, "I will be able to do 25 pushups a day."

♪ *Why* do you want to achieve these goals?
  □ For example, "I want my students to go to a festival where they will get feedback from clinicians who will reinforce what I'm teaching them in class," or, "I don't want my arms to jiggle when I conduct."

♪ *What* is *getting in your way* of achieving these goals?
  □ For example, "Taking my students to a jazz festival requires a lot of paperwork, money, and time," or,

"I don't have the energy to work out after teaching all day."

♪ What are *three* things you could do to move you toward one of these goals?
  - Go to your calendar and write down three separate activities you will do in the next week to help you reach one of these goals.
  - For example, you could write, "1 pushup on Monday, 2 pushups on Tuesday, and 3 pushups on Wednesday."

The idea is to look at your overall goals and then break them down into manageable steps so you're more likely to reach your milestones. In my next chapter, you'll get plenty of practice implementing these strategies, so enjoy the process.

Chapter 7:

Step 4

SNaP Strategies for Music Teachers

Start Now and Progress – or SNaP to it – are strategies I've developed to help change or create behaviors in a hurry. In the next chapter, we will be diving into evaluating and redesigning the first four minutes of your daily class routine so you can maximize your students' learning, engagement, and retention. But, before we do that, I want to take a little bit of time to explore how it is we most effectively go about changing habits for ourselves and how we teach other people to change their habits. That way, when it comes to teaching students these new skills I'm introducing in the next chapter, you'll have some ideas of ways you can teach them the skills that make it easy for them to learn and retain the content you are teaching them. I'm going to

81

offer what may feel like silly suggestions that you might be tempted to skip over, but these little exercises are simple ways for you to understand how to teach yourself or others to break a bad habit, create a new habit, or up-level how you do something. Once you master the ability to effectively do that, everything becomes easier.

Almost everyone learns best when they do it in manageable chunks. That's just a fact of life. When I was a kid (and a young teacher), I "practiced" and "rehearsed" by playing music over and over rather than stopping and working on the things that were hard. Often, what I was really doing was practicing the wrong notes and bad habits over and over, thereby reinforcing them instead of properly mastering a skill before trying to play an entire piece. My mother used to call this "plowing through the music" instead of practicing. It was hard to make any kind of predictable progress when I took this approach.

On the other hand, when I finally wised up and learned how to break things down into smaller components, I could effortlessly master the small skill sets, and the bigger pieces began to fall in place much more accurately and with greater ease. It takes time to figure out how to break the bigger goals down and it takes discipline to routinely practice the new habits, but as a music teacher, you already know the benefits of practicing in this way. The same technique holds up whenever you are trying to learn a new skill, build a new habit, or replace a bad habit, whether that's for you as an individual or when you are teaching students.

Often, when we have a lofty goal, we try to jump directly to it without doing the work to get there rather than planning the steps we can take to reach that goal. I'm guilty of this, that's for sure. There were many occasions I passed out a new tune to the jazz band that I was super stoked for them to play. Inevitably, the lead trumpet part would be a major third higher than Freddy, my lead trumpet player, could comfortably play. But, in my exuberance, I passed out the tune and we went for it. In the learning process, Freddy would miss the notes at first, but given time (and enough pressure on his lips), he'd squeak out those high Cs, and I'd pat myself on the back for being such a great teacher because the band was playing this awesome chart.

But then we'd get to the performances, and it became obvious that he really didn't have the solid range or endurance he needed to consistently (and with good tone) play in that tessitura. He missed notes or stopped playing altogether because his chops got so tired or nerves would take over and he'd default to old habits. I was really causing him more long-term harm than good. He didn't really learn how to extend his range and play well. Instead, he learned how to use bad habits (pressure and more pressure) to squeak out notes that could have come easily if I taught him how to properly and gradually build up his endurance.

I found it was much more effective to help students build their range one small step at a time if I wanted them to truly develop as musicians. Instead of trying to force something out of a horn using techniques that either caused bad habits to form or that weren't dependable for long-term use before they were ready, I began teaching kids how to build their range a half-step at a time. In a matter of weeks, students built the muscles in their embouchures so they can reliably and consistently nail those pitches. By adding just one half-step at a time until it becomes an easy part of the student's range, kids like Freddy can build a foundation that rapidly allows for growth. Before you know it, those high Cs are popping out with good tone, pitch, and consistency – all without putting pressure on his chops and causing damage to his facial muscles!

It doesn't take as long to build a habit or skill as you might think. It does, however, take a clear intention (goal) and persistence (consistency) in order to see the results you want.

I remember losing seventy-five pounds and feeling really good about my body, except for one thing. Every time I was conducting and cut the band off, my upper arms would continue flapping. I hated that. But when you lose a lot of weight, that's one of the "perks." So, I decided to do something about it.

All my life, I've had physical challenges that kept me from being athletic or in shape. Due to arthritis and other issues in my skeletal system, from the time I was a kid, doctors advised me to "take it easy, don't do athletics, and drop out of PE," right before sentencing me to five years in a back brace all through middle school and high school. (I now realize that was *horrible* advice, but back in the 1970s, that's how they "treated" the chronic pain I had.)

Anyway, until I was fifty-one years old, I avoided exercising, but as I began to take control of my health and become empowered to figure out how to be healthier, I realized I was capable of far more physical activity than I ever believed. So, rather than continue being passive about my movement, I became addicted to yoga. That got me in really good shape, but my upper arms still insisted on jiggling, so I decided to do something about it once and for all.

On April 1, 2019, I made the commitment to do a pushup. *One* pushup. It was the longest five minutes of my life! I was shaking as I tried to push myself away from the ground, beads of sweat forming above my eyebrows, imagining my arms giving out with me plummeting (twelve inches) face-first to the ground. It was hard. But I did it. Just one pushup.

On April 2, I did *two* pushups. They were both really hard and I was pretty sure I had reached my maximum potential for the number of reps I'd ever be able to do.

But on April 3, I set out to do three pushups. On this particular morning, the first pushup wasn't quite as hard as my first pushup was on April 1, but the next two more than made up for it.

As each day progressed, I added one more pushup. Predictably, the more pushups I did, the easier it was to do more and more of them. By the time Tax Day rolled around on April 15, I was up to fifteen pushups! That was huge. I went from barely being able to do one pushup just two weeks before to suddenly being able to do fifteen. Sure, the last four or five were difficult, but the first ten were consistently doable without too much effort because my body was being trained to do this new movement and it was becoming a habit.

I was seeing results in my arms, so I was highly motivated to continue. On April 16, I could have done sixteen pushups, but I decided to stick with fifteen ... but about an hour later, I did a *second set* of fifteen pushups, so by April 16, I did thirty pushups in one day! Now I was seeing exponential growth. So, when April 20 rolled around, I added *another* set of fifteen pushups and was up to forty-five pushups a day. On April 30, I added a fourth set, bringing my daily pushup total to sixty pushups. By April 1 of 2020, just one year after starting this push-up extravaganza, I established a daily routine of completing 100 push-ups each morning. No more jiggly arms for this girl!

By taking small, incremental steps that built upon what I did each day before, I was able to take a skill that was very difficult for me on April 1 and do it *sixty* times just thirty days later. Can you imagine what happens when you build your students' skills like that, or when you do your own learning in bite-sized increments? It's almost impossible to fail.

In my first book, I refer to this process as SNaP Strategies. SNaP stands for Start Now and Progress, meaning that you start with one small but manageable task or skill and take small but easy-to-accomplish steps you need to take to reach your goal.

What I love about SNaP Strategies is that they allow you to practice the art of changing, learning, or replacing a habit in ways that focus more on the concept than content so you can later apply the concept in a variety of situations. It's a lot like teaching our students to play scales and etudes. They don't perform those in concerts, but it's through the deliberate attention to the details in those exercises that they learn to hone their muscle memory and skills without all the distractions they'd find if you gave them a piece of literature that required them to implement too many skills they weren't taught yet.

In my exuberance of wanting to share great music with my students, I often gave them literature that was not well-matched to their cognitive or physical abilities or skills. It's frustrating for everyone. That would have been the same as me trying to do sixty push-ups on April 1, 2019 with no incremental steps in going from zero to sixty in thirty days.

There's no way I could have safely done that, but I could do it in thirty days when I planned it out and consistently practiced that skill in small increments.

Whether you are trying to change a habit, learn a new skill, or master new techniques, there are ways of making this happen much faster for yourself and your students. The quickest way to do that is to build the "how-to-learn" muscle, and that is done by intentionally directing attention at a goal and the incremental steps you are going to take to get there... and then taking those steps consistently.

As you think about your classes and what you want your students to know and be able to do as a result of your on-fire teaching abilities, you'll want to become a master at making this warp-speed growth happen. You can practice it by implementing some simple SNaP strategies now so you are making it a daily habit to retrain your brain and your kids' brains. Then, when it comes time to getting your students on board with your new and improved classroom atmosphere, you'll have more strategies for helping them adopt new habits quickly.

Homework Alert

On the following pages are some SNaP Strategies you might want to consider as ways to practice learning how to change behaviors or create a new habit quicker and more effectively than in the past. Make a commitment to doing a strategy for at least a week, then be curious and ask yourself a few questions about what you observed.

Write your observations in a journal so you can see what changes over time.

1. What did I notice when I did this strategy?
   When you do this activity, just be aware of how you feel when you are doing it. Does it make you happy, anxious, peaceful, or bloated? Just notice.

2. What was hard about it?
   Were you tempted to not do it sometimes? What brought resistance?

3. What was rewarding?
   Did it feel particularly good to do the activity, or was the result of doing it something you'd like to experience again?

4. Do the results align with my personal/professional goals or do they distract me?
   Remember, you prioritized those goals in the previous chapter, so hold yourself accountable to doing actions that support you in achieving your goals.

5. Do I want to keep this behavior, modify it, or replace it?
   When I was struggling with my health and realized many of my conditions were due to food sensitivities, I had to figure out what foods were exacerbating my symptoms, so I began noticing how I felt after eating certain foods. It wasn't long before I noticed a direct correlation between consuming gluten and my joint pain – when I ate gluten, I was in constant pain. When

I didn't eat gluten, my joints didn't hurt, and I lost a lot of weight without changing anything else, and my ADHD symptoms improved drastically. I liked how I felt when my body didn't hurt and my brain worked better, so as hard as it is to avoid gluten, it's a behavior I will continue because I am motivated to feel good.

If you like the changes you are seeing, then you may want to continue the new habit or behavior. If you don't like the changes or they aren't worth the effort, then you can at least use the questions above to enlighten you about what you learned from the experiment. When you practice this kind of intentional attention to the little things, the big things become much easier to accomplish.

Here are some ideas of SNaP Strategies for busy band directors. These are just a few suggestions – you can be as creative as you want to be with what you want to do. **The point is to deliberately set a goal and break it down into small steps you can take every day to help you get there sooner.**

SNaP Strategy #1: Gratitude for the Attitude: You find what you look for, 100 percent of the time. So, if you want students who are polite, respectful, engaged, helpful, attentive, and enthusiastic, then look for those qualities in the kids who are right there in front of you every day. They may be difficult to see amongst the distractions that draw your attention away, such as the disruptive students and other responsibilities that get in the way of you noticing the kiddos who always come to class and try to do what you want them to do, but they are there.

When you identify and acknowledge the behaviors you want to see continue, you get more of those – just like when you identify and acknowledge the behaviors you don't want, those become the prevalent behaviors.

Here's what I mean by that statement. Did you ever have a student who was disruptive, so you talked to him, contacted parents, sent an email to the counselor, and finally went to the principal because you were at the end of your rope? Every day, you could make a list a mile long about all the things Max was doing to be disruptive. It's so obvious to you – you notice him as he comes in the room loudly, takes too long to get set up, and never seems to be ready to play when you want him to be, but when you don't want him to play, he's playing. No matter where you move him, he talks to the people next to him, distracting them from being engaged in your riveting rehearsal. He seems to suck up all your attention and energy, diverting it from the other twenty-nine (or sixty) kids in the classroom.

As hard as it seems, what if you could shift your attention (even for a moment) to look for the kinds of behaviors you wanted to see more of, such as Myah going out of her way to put away extra music stands at the end of rehearsal, Ryan helping a new student find music, or Emily asking if she can come in at lunch so she can show you how she finally mastered playing pedal tones on her trombone? Could you find something positive that is going right in just about every class? Or, could you find something Max does that *doesn't* drive you crazy? Anything? Look for it. You'll find something if you look hard enough.

Every day before you leave school, make it a point to acknowledge one student for doing something you want to see continue. I suggest doing it in the form of an email so it can be saved. This is an exercise that has several purposes. It forces you to look for something positive amongst the chaos. When you know you are going to be looking for something positive, you'll have a different mindset. At first it will be hard to do, especially when it feels like you're drowning in overdrive; but when you practice looking for the positive, it becomes easier.

Sending an email to the student's parents, principal, counselor, or any adult who the student and parent would be proud to hear good news from is a way for that student to know that the people who are there to support him are also sharing in his accomplishments. Sending notes like this has a fabulous ripple effect. Even if you only got a glimpse of a positive behavior from a student, if it was there and you acknowledge it and that child gets positive feedback from you, his parents, and another adult or two who saw the email, then he's going to want more of that, so he'll begin to show you more behaviors like that.

This process is something I look forward to. It's my reward at the end of each workday. It makes me leave work with a smile on my face.

Here's your homework – it should be joyful and take no more than five minutes each day.

1. Each day, be on the lookout for one behavior from a student that you can send a positive email about

2. Before leaving school for the day, send a quick email that's something like this:

To the Parents of Lili
CC: Principal, Counselor, Softball Coach

Hello Ms. Smith:

I wanted to send a quick note to you and let you know how much I appreciate having Lili in our band program. Every day in class, I notice how Lili comes in with enthusiasm, takes responsibility for setting up her own equipment, and is ready to play when class starts. Her active participation makes her such a positive role model for her peers.

I sincerely appreciate having Lili in our music program. Thank you for supporting her so she can be a part of our band family.

Mrs. Moffat

I've been doing this for years because it feels good and I see the benefits as students respond with more of the positive behaviors. It feels good to be the one writing the letter, because I often hear back from a parent about how much it meant to hear from me. I love the "this email will go on the fridge" responses I get from proud parents, but what I didn't really understand was how good it felt to be on the receiving end of a letter like that.

We got a new superintendent in the 2019–2020 school year. On the sixth day of school, he and my principal popped into my classroom and stayed for almost thirty minutes. They watched as my students and I went through our daily routine and then rehearsed *New World Symphony*. It was the third day we played that year. This class has sixty kids in grades nine through twelve who got to see important adults take an interest in what they were doing. The superintendent and principal got a chance to see what our students do every day and I thought it was cool to have administrators who cared enough to spend that kind of time in our classroom. I was impressed.

What really surprised me, though, was receiving an envelope in the mail a few days later. You remember old-school letters, right? Anyway, inside that envelope was a letter from the superintendent. It was just a few sentences long, but because of the fact that he took the time to articulate and write a note letting me know he appreciated what I was doing in my classroom, those few sentences meant a lot. And guess what – he cc'd my principal, and when I was walking down the hall the next day, Mr. Peters said, "Did you see the letter from the superintendent?" Yup – it felt good to have the people I respect recognize what I'm doing in the classroom.

That's how our kids and their parents feel when we share good news. Try it. See how it makes you feel. See how it makes your kids feel. And if you like it, then you've just established a habit that will have an incredible ripple effect on your kiddos and your program for a very long time.

SNaP Strategy #2: Time Stealers: How much time do you spend every day looking for stuff, like the paperwork you just filled out for the upcoming field trip, or your score for *Danzon No. 2*, or the cup of coffee you made three hours ago? If you're like most band directors, your office is a bit disheveled (and maybe even your car, too). I noticed that the state of my desk often reflects the state of my mind, so it becomes a visual reminder for me to slow down when I see my desk becoming overly disorganized.

For a few days, notice how much time you spend looking for things that should be easy to locate. Don't judge yourself; just notice. Are you constantly looking for your keys? Do you walk into a room, wonder why you are there, and waste time standing there, trying to clear your head so you can remember? Do you frantically search for that ASB PO you need in order to get a deposit made for an upcoming festival? Do you find yourself filling out paperwork over and over because you start it and then get distracted and never get it completed? Do you have thirty-six kids standing in your personal bubble asking you to help them find music, fix their broken sax, or get a new reed? Is your physical space cluttered? Estimate how much time you spend in this state of mind (for me, I easily used to spend an hour a day spinning my wheels – feeling like I was working because I was doing things, but mostly I was re-doing things or trying to organize myself to get stuff done.)

SNaP: Pick *one* place (desk, office, car, filing cabinet, etc.) where you find yourself being sucked into wasting time and energy because it's getting in your way. Set aside *five* minutes a day to actively transform the place. Hint: Steps 1 through 3 could be done on three different days for five minutes each as you visualize each of these scenarios. After you've imagined the space being ultra-functional and how that will help you serve your students and maintain your sanity, then Step 4 can be done in five minute increments for as long as needed, until your space is set the way you need it so it and you function at your peak.

1. Imagine what you need that space to *look* like in order for you to function at your best. What kinds of things will you do there? Where will things be stored? What will be in your line of sight? What will be out-of-sight but nearby?

2. Imagine what it will *feel* like in that reorganized space. What will it be like to walk into your office, sit down at a desk that's clutter-free, and work on one item at a time? What will it feel like to actually accomplish the task you sat down to do? How will it feel to do it effortlessly, without the frustration of having to go through piles of papers and other stuff to find the information you need to complete your task?

3. Imagine what is possible when you no longer have the visual clutter to distract you and hinder your creativity. It's like closing down all the apps on your phone that are draining your battery. Visual clutter impedes our learning and adds stress to our days. Visualize "deleting" the visual clutter in your space to free up your energy for other things.

4. Set aside five minutes a day to do something to make the space a closer version of your vision. Five minutes. It might take five days or thirty days to complete the task, but either way, the time will pass. Why not have something improve during that time? What space decluttering would give you the most bang for your buck? Start there. Once you've completed decluttering this space, notice what's changed. If you find that the more organized space allows you to save time, function better, and be less flustered, then you've just had a big win! If it doesn't impact your ability to function, then you'll realize this isn't an important contributor to your stress.

SNaP Strategy #3: Reset Yourself: Whether you're going from home to school or between lunch duty and percussion ensemble, it's difficult to bounce from one situation to another and shift gears. I have a few rituals I do that help me transition quickly and effectively so I can head into a new situation and quickly adjust.

Each morning, when I'd pull into the parking lot, I used to get really annoyed with the world's biggest speed bumps. They irritated me because if I didn't slow down enough, the bottom of my car would sound like fingernails on a chalkboard as the speedbumps scraped the undercarriage of my red Volvo. In an effort to protect my car, even though I was in a hurry to get into my classroom, I'd begrudgingly slow down enough to get my mom-car over the bumps without taking out an axle.

A couple of years ago, I thought about the purpose of the speed bumps (other than to annoy me). They were put there to force people to slow down and check their surroundings so they can make sure it's safe before they continue. It's a simple concept. But we all know that without the speedbumps there to provide "incentive" (in the form of not ruining our cars), most people won't slow down. That's how accidents, mistakes, and time-wasting happen. When we don't take the time to check our surroundings, double-check our work, or make sure we are setting ourselves up for success, we run the risk of things going wrong.

I finally came to the realization that speedbumps are actually a good thing. Those oversized and irritating concrete nuisances serve a very important purpose. They'd undoubtedly saved hundreds of lives as careless kids with their heads in their phones cross the parking lot without looking for cars and countless moms behind the wheel with curlers in their hair as they drop off their kids at school "glanced" at their phones as they drove through the parking lot toward those wayward teenagers. Those speed bumps reminded distracted drivers to slow down and be on the lookout and have prevented many tragedies.

How many times a day do you do or say something you wish you could undo? Did you ever do something in a hurry and then realized that if you had taken a moment to think about it, you could have saved yourself a lot of time and frustration? You need to come up with your own "speed bumps." Find something you encounter or do a few times a day – it could be driving over speed bumps or unlocking your classroom door or anything else. Just pick something, and then make a commitment that every time you are in that situation, you reset yourself.

For me, resetting means closing my eyes (or softening my gaze) and taking three deep breaths that extend into every fiber of my body and make me feel like I'm expanding 360-degrees. That act alone slows my heart rate, lowers my blood pressure, and reduces or stops the production of cortisol. I am able, in about sixty seconds, to change my body to go from shooting out toxic hormones that interfere with my health to producing feel-good hormones like dopamine that relax me on the spot. This didn't just happen the first time I took three deep breaths. I had to practice training my brain and body to respond like that, but it didn't take long, and now I can do it on-demand!

I also found that my day starts a whole lot better when I go through my morning routine. Once I pull into my parking space, I get my keys and badge out of the cupholder of my car. While I clip the badge on the waistline of my pants, I simply set an intention of serving my students to the best of my abilities. I know my content is important, but I know my students are more important, and I remind myself to keep that at the core of every action I take and decision I make. As I put my key into my classroom door, I intentionally take a deep inhale and put a smile on my face before turning the key to the right and opening the door.

That might seem silly to mention, but the thirty seconds I spend paying attention to my intention does wonders in helping me remember why I'm doing this important work. When I put a smile on my face, it automatically makes me feel good because the act of smiling signals our brains we are happy, which, in turns, causes our bodies to produce hormones that make us actually *feel* happy. Since I no longer teach the zero-period jazz band, I walk in my room while they are rehearsing. Because I intentionally put a smile on my face before walking in, the kids who notice me coming in the room automatically respond with a smile as a reflex, and that's a pretty awesome way to start every day!

What are your strategies for resetting yourself? Why is it important to have this ability? How can you see your next meeting or parent conference going differently if you were able to decompress yourself before going into those types of stressful situations?

Think of something you do several times a day, such as unlocking your classroom door. Make a commitment that every time you do that action, you will intentionally take another action. For example, every time you unlock your classroom door, you will intentionally take a deep breath and put a smile on your face. If you intentionally do that for 21 days, you will find that it becomes habit to smile when you unlock your classroom door. That means your body and mind will automatically be put in a positive state as your happy hormones get released and override your cortisol. It takes practice, but once you master this ability, you physically feel your heart rate decrease, depth of breath increase, and a sensation of relaxation will take place. That simple act of resetting sets you up to move forward in a different frame of mind, one that is a little less stressed and a lot more likely to help you be a calm teacher.

Identify your "speedbump" of choice, that action that will signal you to slow down and regroup, and then make it an intentional habit to take a few seconds to reset each time you are in that situation. Be sure you use your journal to reflect on what you observed and how you felt when you adopted the new habit.

Like my exercise with pushups, you can invest just a few concentrated minutes a day to support yourself in being more productive or learning a new skill or creating a positive habit, and then you've got a whole new capacity for functioning at a higher level. But more important than the clean office or organized filing cabinet is the process you just went through of identifying a goal and achieving it in incremental but consistent steps. This is how the most effective learning happens in kids and adults. It's biological, so don't fight it. Embrace it. Learn how to teach yourself to effortlessly change habits by using

Chapter 8

Step 5

Tuning Our Bodies

Now that you took the Music Teacher Mojo Meter, understood the importance of the Three Cs (Care, Clarity, and Consistency), identified your personal and professional goals, tried some innovative strategies for changing behaviors, it's time to get to the most transformational component of teaching.

Before I dive in and explain what I'm talking about, I need you to think about a few things. Have an honest chat with yourself for a moment about how you feel when you are teaching. Actually, think about how you feel on Sunday night as you anticipate all of your responsibilities and the things you need to accomplish in the next week. Do you look forward to the week with unbridled excitement like a kid on Christmas Eve, or do you love the idea of changing kids' lives through the magic of music education but also recognize the energy it's going to take to get it all done and start feeling exhausted before you even step into the week?

Do you have both excitement and dread as you think about what you have to do and how much active energy it takes to manage all your students, their parents, the email (my God, there's a lot of email), your inventory, curriculum, meetings, bus duty, field trip planning, and the delivering of engaging and rigorous lessons?

When you're teaching classes, are your students engaged with what you want them to do, or do you constantly feel like you're playing whack-a-mole as you keep them all managed while also trying to provide meaningful instruction? Does thinking about teaching "that one class" tie your stomach in knots? Do you find yourself constantly telling students to "sit down and be quiet," "stop talking," or "put your %^&#$% phone away?" Are you worn out from the active classroom management it now requires to teach music?

If this feels familiar, then I can assure you I relate to how you feel, and I know how to change things. I was great at classroom management, but for me, it was a matter of me being in control of how the kids behaved. I was like a skilled juggler who masterfully kept the percussionists from engaging in making paper airplanes while working with the flutes on a technical passage and telling the trumpet players to look ahead in their music and be ready to play the next part for me and getting the trombones to stop dumping their spit on one another and taking the note the office TA brought for a student's early dismissal and writing a pass for a kid who was about to barf while reminding a third of the class to put their phones away – the list goes on and on. I was monitoring what felt like an infinite number of activities just to be able to get the kids to stay on task. My brain and body were constantly being bombarded with stimulation. That's an exhausting space from which to teach. It's not a great place from which to learn, either. But it was the only way I knew to keep the kids focused and on-task.

Then, my health issues forced me to make some changes in how I ran my classes so I could function as I was coming off of all the prescription drugs I was on for decades, including meds for ADHD, depression, and anxiety, among others. Coming off these meds and having the responsibility for classroom control was a horrible combination – it was just too much stimulation and overwhelm when I had a new batch of students coming in hour after hour, day after day. Managing my symptoms in that environment was going to be incredibly challenging, and I would likely slip back into my old habits if I didn't actively do something to counteract all the overstimulation and worry.

Without the use of medications, I was terrified that I'd lose all sense of focus and control, so I needed to figure out a way to fundamentally change my classroom to a place where rehearsals ran the way I imagined them when I fantasized about being the perfect band director: students are focusing on whatever task is at hand, hanging on to my every word, responding the first time I ask questions, never being distracted by phones or talking, and managing their own behavior so all I have to do is teach music. But that wasn't possible in today's world... or was it?

After a lot of research, best practice, and trial and error, I realized that the problem wasn't what I was teaching or how I was teaching our content. It was *how I was preparing my students to receive, retain, and reuse the information and skills I wanted them to understand.* All their lives, kids are told to sit down and be quiet, but no one really teaches them *how* to do that. We just expect them to do it. After we give them devices and phones and video games and all kinds of other electronic devices that stimulate them constantly, we expect that our simple request to shut it all off and pay attention to us should be easy to follow and we should be able to move on and start teaching.

But that's not how it really works in the classroom, is it?

Heck, it probably doesn't work well for most adults these days, either.

In spite of the best-designed and delivered lesson plans, there are kids who just can't get what we're trying to teach them. Their brains and bodies simply aren't physically or physiologically ready to absorb what we are trying to impart to them. There are too many other thoughts and stimuli taking their attention away from what we're delivering.

Let me illustrate my point with a couple of stories.

Imagine a Thanksgiving dinner where you were invited to a friend's house for a big meal. As you arrive at the house, you walk up to the door, knock, and are immediately greeted by your enthusiastic friend. She wraps you in a big, warm hug, takes your coat, tosses it on a chair, and quickly escorts you into a living room full of people. She loudly announces over the talking of the guests, "Hey everyone, this is Lesley. Lesley, this is everyone." Before you have a chance to ask her a question or get your bearings, she hurries off to greet the next guest. You awkwardly meander around the room, pretending to do something important on your phone in order to avoid eye contact with all these people you don't know.

A few minutes later, your friend returns and invites you to the buffet table, where she proceeds to extend her hospitality by getting a plate and beginning to fill it up for you. She wants you to feel welcome, so she narrates as she piles your plate high with all the goodies. "You'll love Janie's sweet potatoes, they're delicious with her secret ingredient," and, "Jennifer's green bean casserole is soggy. You'll hate it." As she gives you all the information you need so you don't have to make your own decisions about what food you like or don't like or how much of it to dish up, she happily pours gravy all over your mashed potatoes and turkey (you hate gravy) and salts *everything* on the plate, and you are handed a plate full of what she picked for you. She walks you over to a table and puts you between two people you never met and then goes to talk to other guests. As you sit down and look at your plate, you see a hodgepodge of food, some of which you want to try and other stuff that isn't at all appealing. But there it is, and somehow, you're expected to enjoy this feast.

Now, imagine that as soon as you take the last bite of your dinner, a piece of pumpkin pie with whipped cream is placed in front of you. No one asked you if you are dairy-free, but it would be rude not to eat it, so now you face the dilemma of either not eating what you're served or eating something you know will make you sick. As soon as dinner is over, imagine your friend handing you your coat as she escorts you out of the door while reminding you of everything you just ate, the people you just met, and then telling you to have a nice day. Whew! How would you feel? Full? Uncomfortable? Overwhelmed? Would your body feel good after eating a meal someone else piled on your plate without regard to your likes, dislikes, or dietary needs? Did you have quality conversations in a noisy and chaotic environment like that where you didn't get a chance to have a meaningful connection with any of the other guests? Would any of this create anxiety for you? Would you be able to remember details about the meal, people you met, or things you talked about if you experienced a situation like that?

How many of us teach like that? I know I did – for a very long time, and I was praised for it. I believed I was doing the best possible teaching because I actively involved as many of the students' senses as possible so I could incorporate multiple ways for them to experience what they were learning. Let me explain.

When I exposed students to a piece of music for the first time, I had a routine we would always use for sight-reading. Once the new sheet music was passed out and I was assured every kid had a pencil on his or her music stand, our process went something like this.

I would tell the students all about the music: who composed it; what makes it a good piece; why the composer wrote it; what the composer wants them to feel; what part they should like best (where to build up); how they should interpret the music; everything they should do and think so they didn't have to make any mistakes or decisions on their own

Students then took their pencils and *marked all "important" spots,* which meant I had them circle all key signatures, time changes, dynamics, and other musical indications before we sight-read the music so we could preempt any mistakes we might make. Students would *listen* to a high-quality audio recording of the piece, and they would hold their instrument in playing position and "play" along to the recording, and I would conduct from the podium, and the list went on and on.

Next, students would mark anything that caught them off-guard as we listened to the recording, and I expected students to keep an eye on me while I conducted along to the recording and shouted out rehearsal numbers in case someone got lost as we did silent band karaoke.

I gave the students everything they needed to be successful, and then I'd be baffled when we would play the music for the first time without the recording and they didn't crescendo the way they heard it on the recording I just played for them *and* the way it was written in their music with dynamics *and* the fact that I had them circle the crescendo with a pencil. How could they not be successful when I was so helpful in providing so much high-quality and important information for them? It didn't make sense to me. Then they'd get frustrated, and so would I. I didn't understand why, when I was engaging so many of their senses at the same time giving them so much information, they were getting overwhelmed and frustrated. That resulted in disruptive behaviors, as kids would disengage from the overstimulating environment I was providing.

This situation reminds me of the Thanksgiving dinner I described. In both scenarios, the person coming into the environment (you as the guest or your students in your classroom) is being overstimulated by sights, sounds, and other sensory-arousal activities that are naturally present when transitioning from one environment to another, and all that stimulation interferes with the ability to take in whatever content is being offered. It takes people a little bit of time to enter, assess, and adjust to the energy of a new space. **Skipping the step that allows them to acclimate and sync with their surroundings means that residual energy from whatever is already on their mind and in their bodies is still there and will interfere with whatever comes next.**

If you are full after a big meal and someone is trying to get you to eat more food, especially if it's something you don't really like, you don't even want them to put a plate in front of you because you know you don't have the capacity to take it in. Likewise, if you're collapsed on the couch after over-eating and you feel the waistband of your pants digging into your belly as your brain goes into a food coma, the last thing you'll want to do is engage in an activity that requires you to be physically or mentally alert.

The same principle holds true with our brains and learning new information. When I was giving my students *everything* I thought they needed to be "successful" in music, I was actually taking away the power of the music to speak directly to the kids themselves. I got in the way and it hindered their progress. When I took kids who were already over-stimulated from being teenagers in the twenty-first century and then put their brains and bodies into overdrive and expected them to take in all of this new information without making room for it, they simply didn't have the capacity to process everything I was throwing at them, so they'd end up not retaining much of it in the end.

Let's go back to Thanksgiving, but this time imagine you're invited to a different friend's house the next year. Not wanting a repeat of the Thanksgiving from hell you experienced last year, you accept this invitation, but your hopes aren't too high.

As you get out of your car and walk up the long driveway, a gentle snow begins to fall, dusting everything with a fresh coat of winter white peacefulness. You notice how cozy the house looks as the soft golden glow of the lights shines through the windows and a trail of smoke curls lazily out of the fireplace. Just before you knock on the door, you hear the sounds of glasses clinking, cheerful holiday music playing, and people laughing, and a minute later, your friend opens the door and welcomes you in with a warm hug.

After taking your coat and hanging it up in the closet, she ushers you into the living room, where other friends are gathered around the tree, sharing some light snacks and conversation. She takes you to a group of them and introduces you to each person, sharing little tidbits of information about what you have in common or something of interest, before excusing herself to greet another guest.

Following some lighthearted conversation with your new friends, you all make your way to the buffet, but this year, you get to pick up your own plate and serve yourself. You get to decide how much turkey to pick and whether or not you want gravy on your potatoes. If you don't like green beans, then you can skip that option altogether. You are assured that you can return to the table again and again, so rather than trying to take in everything on the first trip through, you are able to enjoy small amounts of foods and then go back for more if you're still hungry.

After you've finished a relaxing meal that had food you enjoyed and conversation with people you got a chance to know, imagine being offered different options for dessert so you could determine if you wanted it or not; and, if you weren't ready right away, you knew you could go back for it when you were ready.

Then imagine that after a lovely and leisurely meal, you had time to talk and connect before your friend walked you to the door, thanked you for being there, and said she couldn't wait to see you again soon.

If you were asked to describe the two Thanksgiving meals, you'd be likely to give far more details about the setting, context, meal, feelings, and people you met in the second scenario than in the first because you were given the opportunity to take in all of the new information *after* being "synchronized" with the other guests.

What do you think would happen in a classroom where you operated from a place like this second meal? What if your students were invited into your classroom and given an opportunity to decompress from whatever they were doing before coming to your class prior to being bombarded with everything you want to teach them? How might that impact the way they receive what you're teaching, how well they retain it, and how they're able to reuse that information in new and creative ways?

I began to explore teaching from the same mindset as the second Thanksgiving dinner I described. What I mean by that is that I shifted from the overstimulating and over-delivery type of teaching to one where I presented information to students in a way in which they could digest it better. The results of shifting to this kind of teaching are nothing short of miraculous.

Instead of continuing to give my students the "right answers" about music and hoping they remembered everything, I began to restructure how I prepared them for class. Before bombarding them with the content of the day, I learned how to help them transform their bodies and brains to be biologically prepared for band. I created a protocol we use in every class every day for the first four minutes, and after just a few weeks, I began to see remarkable changes.

Students became much more attentive and engaged in what we were doing... but without me being so actively involved in keeping them quiet, motivated, and on-task. When they learned how to shed the thoughts from whatever happened in the class before and tune-in to band, our collective musicality and artistry soared because they were becoming more immersed in the music.

When our daily four-minute routine is used each day, our collective heart rates become more unified, our breathing becomes deeper and more accessible, and our head-chatter begins to diminish. The classroom culture becomes one where students are emotionally much more even keeled and feel at ease with their peers.

For many decades in my classroom, I thought I didn't have time to spend on anything that didn't directly help my students play music better. After all, that's how music teachers are often judged – by the scores and the quality of music their students put out. What I failed to realize is that I could help them become better musicians if I actually took the time to invest in setting up the atmosphere, their brains, and their bodies so the time we spent learning new skills could be more productive. My teaching was good, but it was because I spent so much time and energy keeping kids focused, planning engaging rehearsals and lessons, and actively doing things to control the atmosphere. I was buying into the theory that we must be instructing kids from bell-to-bell, so anything other than active instruction felt like a waste of time.

I was so wrong.

Once I understood the value in properly preparing my students to be ready to learn, collaborate, and be engaged while managing their own behavior, I knew I struck gold! My classroom went from an overstimulating environment where kids often felt overwhelmed to one where we flowed with ease. It was *so* much easier on the students and on me – and we are all learning so much more than when we "didn't have time" to do anything that wasn't considered rehearsing.

Here's the magic I've been waiting to reveal: When you help students physically and mentally decompress before teaching, they are ready to receive, retain, and reuse the information you are sharing. If you skip that essential step, you're going to work ten times harder for half the results. Guaranteed.

Let me illustrate this with a quick analogy. We live in Seattle, so we get a lot of moss and debris that accumulates during the rainy season (which happens to last a very long time). Dirt, grime, and pine needles seep into all of the surfaces in our yard, from wooden decks and a concrete driveway to a painted deck surface and all the outdoor furniture. We have to pressure wash annually to keep things clean. It's a real pain, but it's part of the maintenance we must do if we want our property to hold up for the long haul.

After pressure washing, we then need to put on different types of treatment in the form of sealant, stain, or paint to protect the surfaces from being damaged by debris that falls on it as the next rainy season approaches.

Pressure washing is a pain and takes a long time. It would be really nice to skip that step and just apply the deck stain, concrete sealer, or paint right away. But if we did that on top of the moss and dirt that had accumulated over the past year, it would be a terrible idea. Not only would the product not stick to the surface and do the job it was intended to do, now we'd also have a heck of a mess as the treatment and dirt combined to create a gooey sludge that would be difficult and disgusting to clean up.

We would waste a lot of time, money, and energy if we took a shortcut like that, and it's pretty obvious that it would be a dumb idea.

I used to teach without "pressure washing" first. I'd give my students lots of content, but I didn't help them make room for it first, so they couldn't effectively receive, retain, and reuse it. In the example of pressure washing, I am reminded of how our students enter our classrooms. They come to us every day with different needs. The needs vary from kid to kid and from day to day. They bring baggage that makes it hard for them to concentrate and learn because they are full of worry and anxiety, depression and ADHD. After the 2020 pandemic and resulting school closures, many more of our kids come to us experiencing the impact of trauma. Some kids come from happy homes and feel great, but they get lost in the shuffle because teachers are busy paying attention to the kids who require more active supervision. Some kids are struggling with their identity, sexuality, and dozens of other confusing situations, yet we bring them into our classrooms and *bam*, we dive into our rigorous bell-to-bell content delivery and wonder why everyone is frustrated and struggling. So, we try harder to help students get it by giving them more of the same, but it becomes futile. All of these things and a million other distractions make it really hard for kids to focus and learn.

When I was pressure washing my deck, driveway, and patio, I quickly learned that each surface needed a different amount of pressure in order to get clean. I have proof that if you use the same intensity of pressure on the soft wood of the deck that you use on the concrete driveway, you'll gouge the wood. Likewise, if you try to clean a concrete surface with the light pressure used on wood, it doesn't have enough power to get that surface clean. Every surface needs to be cleaned off in order to receive the new material, but each surface needs a little different type of help to clear the right amount of clutter and enable it to be most receptive to what we were going to put on it.

This is how our students operate. They need an opportunity to physically and mentally clear away the clutter that gets in the way of them being able to receive what it is we're trying to teach them. They literally need to reset before they can receive, but no one taught them how to actually reset themselves.

They come to us with their bodies and brains jacked up. They were bombarded with stimuli in the halls, at recess, in the lunchroom, on the bus, in other classes, at home, on computers and phones nearly round-the-clock, and yet they go from classroom to classroom being told to sit down, be quiet, and pay attention.

Well, that's really hard to do, so we must teach them how to do it. Then we can teach them anything – anything at all.

Let me repeat this, because it is the whole premise of this entire book and everything I teach: **Before we can teach any of our content, we must "tune our students' bodies and brains" so they are able to receive what we offer. That starts with reversing how we teach.**

We all went to universities and learned how to tell what music was "good" and what was "bad." We became experts at determining when music was being played correctly and when there were mistakes. We learned pedagogy and philosophies. We learned how to present information and scaffold our lessons.

But did anyone ever teach us how to *biologically program our own and our students' brains and bodies for band*? That's what we're about to do, and you aren't going to believe what can happen in *your* classroom!

This is where the First Four Minutes protocol comes in. *What is the First Four Minutes protocol?* It is a routine I began practicing on my own as a way to help me function without ADHD medications. It worked so well for me that I took it into my classroom and shared the practice with my students. The results are nothing short of staggering.

If you'd like a quick explanation of this magical process, check out my ten-minute video that explains the First Four

Minutes protocol and benefits here: https://youtu.be/0b8p-js3Duhk. In a nutshell, the First Four Minutes is a simple routine I devised that invites students to bring their bodies to stillness, settle comfortably into their chairs, and deepen their breath. It's nothing fancy, but over the course of a few minutes, I give them verbal cues to relax from head to toe. Then, I count from one to ten, inviting them to relax even more with each exhale. Within thirty seconds of my starting this routine, students go from having bouncy energy and chattiness to absolute silence and relaxation. In many cases, they look like Raggedy Ann and Andy dolls as their bodies completely relax in their chairs. For so many of them, this is the only time each day when their parasympathetic nervous systems get a chance to move out of fight-or-flight mode and into a state where they are capable of learning, physiologically allowing their bodies to stop shooting out cortisol and instead produce oxytocin and other feel-good hormones. When that happens, their brains literally shift into being able to access the areas that impact enduring learning so students can actually learn and retain what you're about to introduce. Do you see why this is golden?!

But wait... there's more! When you practice doing this with your students every single day, their automatic response to the sound of your voice is to become calm and this relaxation process helps them shift into this learning state quickly and easily in your presence. You can't make this stuff up!

Everything I do during our daily First Four Minute routine biologically resets the students (and me) to be physically and physiologically ready to learn. We literally synchronize our brains and our bodies, settling our energy as we bring stillness into our bodies and allow our breath to become the focus of what we are doing.

Taking the time to set the stage for each class has the same impact on learning as pressure washing has on preparing outdoor surfaces for a fresh coat of paint, because it washes away the clutter and makes room for new input. Here are just a few of the benefits that come from adopting this practice into your daily routine:

- Classroom management becomes effortless
- Students play in tune much better as their bodies become more sensitive to pitch (vibration)
- Students are more musically sensitive and expressive
- Nearly all tardies are eliminated
- Students are much more engaged
- Performance skills improve
- Stress levels are markedly decreased
- Non-instructional noise eliminated/greatly minimized
- Students demonstrate a deeper understanding of what we are learning
- We create a communal energy
- Students and teachers experience reduced heart rates and calming of excess energy
- Students and teachers tap into the intuitiveness of music more than the "gotta-get-it-rightness"
- Kids like the benefits, both personal and as a group, so they are motivated to continue

- Much higher retention rate
- Benefits carry over from year to year

Think for a moment about holding a snow globe. When you gently shake it, the glittery snow begins swirling around the scene inside. If you were to walk around with the snow globe in your hands, the glitter would continue moving about. Only if you physically set the snow globe down and allow gravity to do its thing for a couple of minutes would the snow actually make its way to the bottom of the snow globe to clearly reveal what you want to see.

Now, think about your students as they enter your classroom. Each one is like a piece of the glitter in the globe, with its own energy as it moves into the room, gathers equipment, sets up, interacts with peers, and settles in for your class.

What you do with their combined energy in the next few minutes will determine how receptive and responsive they are to *everything* you do for the rest of the class, from their behavior and artistry to participation and retention. You'll have their undivided and focused attention, and the cooperative learning atmosphere will blow you away.

Once you corral their collective energy, instead of having sixty bodies full of their own random energy, you'll have one ensemble energy, and you can truly work your magic. Much like geese, when our students are left to their own accord, their progress can seem random and hard to control, but when energy becomes focused and unified (for geese, when they assemble to fly in their V-formation; for students, when they unify their heartrates and breathing), progress toward a goal is not only possible, but it's also inevitable. We can see it, communicate it, and guide our students toward it when we take the time to let the energy settle before leading them through the rest of class.

In a nutshell, I talk my students through a body relaxation exercise that incorporates deep breathing and visualization. There's no hocus-pocus or woo-woo stuff going on; just simple responses humans are already biologically pre-programmed to have, such as physically relaxing as they exhale. That's something our bodies are designed to do; but in today's world, we don't teach people how to tap into that ability, so they are fighting all the extra energy – just like how glitter floats around in the snow globe if it isn't given the opportunity to do what nature intended and follow gravity to get out of the way of the scene.

When you practice a routine every day with your students, you help them change behaviors. Synchronizing them as a group every day clears out the clutter within each of them and between them as a group. Spending four minutes unifying their heartbeats (internal metronomes) and settling down their amygdala by allowing them to get out of stress/fight-or-flight mode (which we all seem to live in these days) physically resets them so they can receive what you offer.

This is what I was illustrating with the pressure washing example I gave earlier. Each student comes to us needing different kinds of help in preparing his or her brain and body to take in new information, but regardless of what kind of distractions they have going on in their lives, they all benefit from going through this process.

Music is so interactive, and we all rely on one another in order to be our best ensemble. When we take the time to invest in resetting the entire group, every person in the room benefits.

As music teachers, we rely on our students to express our artistry. With our backs to an audience, we put our reputations in the hands of hundreds of youngsters, asking them to take black dots off a piece of paper and turn them into beautiful sounds that will make people feel emotions. The students essentially become our instruments. Like any instrument from which we expected to get a quality performance, we must take good care of them. Each individual student is like a string on a piano. If we have just one broken string, let's say middle C, but every other string is perfectly tuned, everything we play is still going to be impacted in a negative way because of the one broken string. It simply can't give us what we need, even when we repeatedly hit the key over and over. Now, imagine a student in your classroom who can't focus on what you need him to do to learn and contribute to the ensemble's progress. Perhaps something in his life is so broken that the thoughts in his head and nervous energy in his body simply won't let his mind or muscles respond in the way either of you want him to. Those distracting thoughts limit his capacity to decompress so he can access a learning state. Not only does it make it hard for him to learn, but it hinders the rest of the ensemble, too. You can help him and every other kid in your classroom reset every day in your presence so they can be the best versions of themselves and respond as the prized instruments you know they are.

Let me caution you – this is not a one-and-done experience. You don't take students through this process once, twice, or occasionally and see major changes any more than you would expect your lead trumpet player in jazz band to practice a range-building exercise for a day or two and then magically have the muscles built up to support a range that is a perfect fifth higher with good tone and reliability.

The power of this protocol comes in the way in which you design and implement it and the consistency with which you practice it. Training our bodies and brains to learn how to relax and reset is a skill that can be learned through intentional practice.

Every day, our kids leave us and don't return for twenty-four or more hours. During that time, life happens. Different experiences happen to everyone in the class, and when they return the next day, there are new sets of stressors and triggers that impact them. By repeating this protocol with them in our classrooms every day, we begin to train their muscle memory and the process of getting them fully relaxed and reset in our presence becomes an automatic response, regardless of the extra baggage they bring in the form of distractions.

But who has time to add something else to an already too-packed schedule?

At first, I was tempted to skip this practice on days when we had short class periods or we were getting close to a concert because I wanted to maximize my rehearsal time, but what I found was that we *saved* significantly more rehearsal time when we invested four minutes in this synchronization because our rehearsals became uber-efficient as excess distractions were eliminated and students became focused on our collective goals when we did our routine and they were all brought into the focus together.

It's like brushing our teeth. We don't brush our teeth on Monday mornings and then consider it to be sufficient for getting us through the week. That would be ridiculous, because we know that every time we eat, we are accumulating bits of stuff that creates bacteria and bad breath. It feels gross, and we wouldn't imagine spending our days with the microbes multiplying in our mouth.

Our brains and bodies need to be reset each day, too. As music teachers, we are in the perfect position to teach students this valuable skill. I already shared many of the benefits we discovered since implementing this in my classes and with the directors I coach through Band Director Boot Camp, and the results work with students from every walk of life and at all ages.

But here's the best news of all: When you have a process where you have gotten your students in a relaxed and ready-to-learn state, there are two things guaranteed to happen for the rest of the class period:

1. The students will continue to hear your voice.

2. The students will continue to breathe.

Your voice and them breathing are now triggers for them to be calm and relaxed in your presence!

Can you imagine how easy it is to teach when your students have the opportunity to calm down, de-escalate, and reset for your class? Can you imagine what it's like when they are surrounded by a room full of their peers who are also calm, de-escalated, and reset for class? It's utterly amazing, because when you help your students feel better, you can help them do anything.

One of my clients, Chelsey, a middle school band director in the Midwest, created her own First Four Minutes protocol using this process. She contacted me in August as she was getting ready to return for another school year. Her son was a year and a half old, and she told me that while she loved her job, it sucked every ounce of energy out of her because of the active management it took to run all of her classes. "Ms. E, where's the valve oil?" "Josh just threw up on his trumpet." "I can't come to the concert tonight, Ms. E, but that doesn't hurt my grade, does it?" She was exhausted before she even got to the actual instructional part of her day. She told me how the first ten to fifteen minutes of class consisted of getting everyone set up and organized. It was really cutting into instructional time and leaving her frazzled. The routine was wearing her out.

She and I worked together to take what I do in my class and customize it to serve her students' needs. What she came up with looks different than what I do in my classroom, but it serves the same purpose. It sets aside time when everyone resets their bodies and brains, clearing out the clutter that would otherwise manifest as outbursts, distractions, inability to focus, inability to remember, difficulty following directions, and more as class progressed. A few months later as we were about to head back to school after the winter holiday break, Chelsey sent me a text. Considering how frazzled she was feeling as she anticipated the new school year just four months prior to this, I was overjoyed to see how the First Four Minutes protocol she designed transformed her classroom and, therefore, her personal stress levels, energy, and effectiveness as a parent and teacher. Here's part of the text she sent me on the eve of returning to school after winter break:

"Lesley,

Band Director Boot Camp was such a game changer for me. It's helped restore positivity and peace to the culture of my classroom, introduced many significant new protocols that align with our school's theme and mission, and has taken the headache off of me and given responsibility to my students.

We are all operating in a healthier, more efficient classroom where each individual has a role and we feel safe within our four walls. We laugh as a family and I know they'll continue on knowing that band was a place where they belonged."

By creating a format that works for her students' needs and best prepares them for class, she gave her students the tools to self-manage much of their own behavior. The ripple effect when students are taught this kind of skill and they practice it in your presence every day is remarkable.

My template in the next chapter works in much the same way as chord changes for a jazz chart. It provides the structure so you can see what purpose each step serves and then use your own personality and ideas as the teacher and expert in your classroom to decide how you design it, just like you'd use a lead sheet as a guide to create your own solo that reflects your personality and mood and style.

Come with me into the next chapter, where we will dive into the template that outlines the principles of the First Four Minutes, a sample script I use, and a place for you to start creating your personal plan that will work for you and your students in creating a classroom where teaching becomes stress-free and you and your students can focus on making beautiful music together.

Chapter 9:

Step 6

Creating Your Own
First Four Minute Protocol

Now that you had a chance to understand how this process fundamentally transforms your classroom from a teacher-centered active classroom management plan to a student-owned responsibility, you're probably stoked to get it in place.

I will break down the steps for creating your own First Four Minutes plan, and I will also walk you through the steps you need to plan *before* you introduce this to your students. This is where you get to identify the Three Cs of Success (why you *care* about this, be *clear* about what your outcomes are, and *consistently* practice this skill so it becomes habit for your students) so you're able to successfully implement your plan and get the results you desire.

Take the time to write down your responses for each question. They are designed to get you to think about the obstacles and resistance you may face as you design and implement this new strategy. Skipping this step will likely end up with this becoming just another technique you try for a little while then abandon because it's not working the way you wanted it to do.

My most successful clients are the ones who struggle through the hard questions *before* they introduce this to their students so that by the time they are ready to implement it, they have a solid understanding of why it's so important to do it mindfully and consistently and have the commitment to follow through.

If you are going to help your students overcome their biggest barriers to learning, you need to know what those barriers are, so why not ask them? After all, when you ask the people who are most impacted by what happens in the class what makes it hard for them to achieve their goals, then you can begin to create the structure they crave and in which they will thrive.

The manner in which you collect this information is irrelevant. Use a format that helps you get the kind of information you want and need in a way you can access it. A Google survey works great, but so does a class discussion. You're the expert in your classroom as to how you can best get information from your students, so you will need to decide *how* you are going to find out what annoys them the most or keeps them from focusing and engaging in your class.

Once they have an opportunity to voice their challenges and you understand what their barriers are (other students who are disruptive, people being on their phones, people not paying attention, etc.), then you'll be able to share with them how this protocol will help those distractions go away and let them enjoy making music rather than waiting for you to try and get the class quiet every time you stop the band.

So, ask your kids to be honest with what they need. Then, let them know you take your responsibility as their teacher seriously and will do everything in your power to help them reach their goals. That is the whole purpose of why you're doing this. Once your kiddos see that you're all on the same team and you, as their coach, are trying to help the whole team achieve great heights, they're much easier to bring on board. If you simply take this idea and tell your kids to "sit down and breathe with me," they won't have the buy-in because they'll see it as another thing being done *to* them instead of *for* them. Once you understand their challenges, you can better create a First Four Minute plan to serve their needs. Asking for and listening to their voices and concerns helps them see that you are creating a tool for them to help them overcome some of these challenges.

- **What are the things you need to know from your students in order for you to help them understand how this will be something they will want to do?** Examples might include:
  - What interferes with their learning?

- Why do they talk so much?
- Why don't they pay attention more?
- Why are they constantly on their phones?
- Why don't they remember what I tell them?
- What are the external challenges that prevent them from learning (home life, rough classes, food insecurity, etc.)?
- How can I help them be less distracted so they can learn easier?

- **Create a survey or list of questions for a class discussion so you can find out what impedes their learning.** Examples might include:
  - What is the one thing that makes it challenging for you to learn in our class?
  - Are you easily distracted by other students' behaviors?
  - Do you have any behaviors that might distract others?
  - Do electronic devices tempt you even when you try to pay attention?

- **Talk to your students about why you are asking them these questions so they will be honest with you about what they need in order to be successful in your class**

Implementing

This is where *consistency* comes into play. This is the part that's not negotiable. You obviously need to have clear reasons for making a significant change of this magnitude (crystal-clear results you are seeking) and a plan for how you are going to get there, but if you don't practice the new skills on a regular basis, they cannot become habits that serve you even when you're not focused on them.

When you first started learning to conduct, it likely took every bit of your concentration to read the score, follow along, look for and anticipate areas you need to cue, listen to and evaluate what you were hearing and how that jived with what you saw on the score, conduct through changing time signatures and tempi, make sense of all the transpositions and clefs, and get dozens of other people to take the same tempo you wanted to go. You probably failed miserably – many times. But you didn't give up. You assessed what did work and what didn't work and then you got right back up on the podium and practiced some more.

This is the mindset you need as you introduce and implement a strategy like this. At first, it will feel awkward, and the easy thing to do will be to give up. Let me tell you from experience, when I wrote my first book and suddenly found myself in front of cameras and being interviewed, I was beyond awkward. My stomach would twist uncomfortably in knots and I even forgot the title of my own book during one interview! I really wanted someone else to be the one to do all my publicity so I wouldn't have to be uncomfortable in front of other people, but my mentor wouldn't hear of it. She provided templates for marketing, but she insisted that I had to understand my content and my audience and put my own stuff out there. Lots of it failed, but because I knew I needed to reach music teachers with a message that could help them, I had to consistently practice until my skills improved and I could be heard by more people.

You will go through that same resistance with this process at some point. I promise. You will want to quit because it will feel uncomfortable while your students are in the process of learning to adopt this practice. The clients I had who worked through the challenges by assessing how things were going, reworking what was not working, and going back and trying it again are getting unbelievable results with their students, both musically and in the rehearsal setting. But, it takes persistence, just like everything else worth learning.

What good would it do to start to teach your students a chromatic scale and then give up after they learned five consecutive notes? Would you dream of abandoning the teaching and reinforcing of important skills like playing with proper sound, observing key signatures, and being musically sensitive and expect students to somehow magically master those skills with no repeated practice? Probably not. So, approach teaching the skill of relaxing and resetting for a productive learning session with the same diligence and care and you're sure to meet with success.

- *Why* is it important for you and your students to take the time to regroup and reset before digging into rehearsal? This is your *one* sentence elevator speech you'd use if a colleague were to say to you, "I heard you have your kids do an activity every day at the beginning of your class. Why?" What would you tell that teacher as to why you are so adamant about investing four minutes per class period on this technique? What are the *results* you want for your students and your own peace of mind? My rationale is, *"My classes are easy and fun to run because my students and I are literally tuned into the same mental and physical frequency, just like our instruments need to be in tune in order for us to play well together."* Write your sentence down. Memorize it. Feel it. Believe it.

- *How* **will you introduce this protocol to your students?** When I first introduced this to my students, I shared my own personal story about my struggle with ADHD, depression, and anxiety and how that impacted my ability to do my job. I also told them that I was coming off all the medication I took to help me with the symptoms of these conditions so I needed to find other ways of helping me cope with the symptoms that would still be there. I shared with them how spending a few minutes quietly resetting my brain and body became the tool I used to achieve the same focus I used to only be able to get from pills. I explained that I needed to use that technique to reset between classes or else I would be so distracted that I wouldn't be a very good teacher because it was a real struggle. I told them that since it was so helpful for me, I wanted to share it with them.

They are kind and cooperative human beings, so they did it with me, even though it felt weird at first. By sharing my personal reason and the benefits I got from doing this, they could see I genuinely wanted the same kind of results for them, and that made it easier to get them on-board.

You may not want to share such a deeply personal reason. That's fine. Just be sure you think about how you will talk about this process with your students and how you'll talk about your expectations so they'll understand what the outcome will be and how it will benefit them. The thing that matters most is whether or not you are sincere.

How do you plan on helping your students see the value in this process? How will you explain that to your students in a meaningful way that gets them to understand and buy-in to this process?

- *What* **delivery method will you use?** I do my First Four Minutes via verbal cuing. I simply talk the students through a relaxing body scan and deep breathing.

  Chelsey's students' needs are different than my students' needs, so she designed her process a little differently by recording herself cuing the relaxation exercise and then adding background music and a video that she shows that helps students pace their breathing to match the visual cues, which still results in helping them reduce their heart rates and physically calm down. That works magically in her situation.

I also worked with teachers who aren't comfortable doing the breathing exercises in their classes yet, so they use guided listening with music that helps students relax before diving into instruction. Other clients used a combination of movement and music to get their students centered and focused.

Think about your students, classroom set up, equipment, and other variables and then decide the simplest way to deliver it in that context.

- **_When_ will you introduce this to your students?** Walking into your classroom tomorrow with grandiose plans of implementing this before you took the time to create it and plan on rolling it out will result in it not being effective. If you really want to make a significant change in how you teach and how your students learn, you need time to think through your current routine and your desired results and plan how to implement this before introducing it to your class. Decide what day you will start (give yourself adequate time to prepare - one week to two months is ideal) and then make a commitment to that start date by writing it in your planning book or calendar.

Obstacles

In spite of your best intentions, detailed planning, scrupulous attention to detail, and clear vision, there will be obstacles that arise in setting this up and getting it to become part of the accepted daily routine by your students. You can't eliminate every obstacle that comes up, but you can be prepared to address and resolve challenges in a way that supports the long-term growth and goals that caused you to implement this new protocol in the first place.

You do that by anticipating the obstacles that could come up and pre-thinking (visualizing) how you will handle the obstacles so that when they do pop up, you're prepared! Your challenges will be different than mine, so you need to ask yourself these questions through the lens of your school, your students, and your community.

- **What will you do when the novelty has worn off and students ask, "Do we have to do this *every* day?"** How do you handle it when kids want to give up when other things become hard or boring or they simply don't understand enough to make a judgement? Were they 100% on-board when you taught them to play a concert Bb scale? Probably not at first, but once they learned it and could do it effortlessly, they reaped the benefits from practicing it by being able to play those patterns easier and more accurately every time they appeared in music they encounter. Even though this is a different topic, it's the age-old idea of continuing through resistance when something new is hard. Approach teaching this concept in the same way you approach teaching all the other important skills you want your students to master.

Ask your students if they reset their phones or computers on a regular basis. What other things do they do regularly in order to get rid of things that they don't need any more (they'll talk about going to the bathroom to get rid of stuff their bodies don't need, brushing their teeth to clear out the grossness, showering to get dirt and perspiration off their bodies, etc.)? Doesn't it make sense that since they accumulate junk in their mouths, on their bodies, and in their bodies, that their brain also accumulates stuff it needs to clear out, too? If they don't take time to physically and mentally reset, it's like having a hundred windows open on their computer and wondering why it's running so slowly.

What analogies or stories can you use to help your students see the connection between practicing this technique and becoming the amazing band family they want to be?

What benefits can you draw their attention to so they are consciously aware of the positives instead of assuming they're making the connections between what you're doing with this routine and the more fun they can have in rehearsals and with the music?

- **How will you prepare admin and parents for this new protocol?** You know your community best, so think about how this new practice could be interpreted and determine if you should talk to your administrator before implementing it or if you want to share it with parents so they are familiar with this process. I always make a point of talking about this at curriculum night so every parent knows exactly what we do and why we do it. When I tell them how this is based on human biology, how it is directly related to helping their kids improve as musicians, and how it can help them in all kinds of other life situations, they understand the value in what I am asking their children to do. The comments I get about how this technique has fundamentally changed their children's mental states of mind never cease to amaze me! I invited my principal, my superintendent, and our district's health and wellness coordinator into my classroom to experience this process so they had firsthand knowledge of what we do. This was an important step in successfully implementing this in my classroom – if a parent were to call an administrator and ask why I'm spending four minutes of class time every day doing something non-instructional or "not band-related," any of these administrators could articulate the value of this exercise. *Who do you need to have on-board so this is successful?*

After you go through all the questions above, you'll be ready to create your own First Four Minutes script. Just like the first attempt at an improvised solo, there will be parts that feel awkward and uncomfortable, but as you think about it and revise it, it will begin to feel as natural as it is for you to stand in front of a room full of kiddos, look at a musical score in front of you, raise your arms, and lead them through a complex piece of music. It took time, practice, and patience to build your own conducting skills, but you stuck with it, and now you can do all those things even while there are distractions like chatty percussionists and cell phones pulling your attention away from the score and your conducting techniques. You trained your brain and body to do those things automatically, and you are about to train your own and your kids' brains and bodies to have the automatic responses of being focused and attentive in your presence. This is too good not to invest in doing right!

Final Product

Once you answer the questions in the preceding section (do it in writing so you really have taken the time to articulate your responses), you will create your own First Four Minutes script using the guide that follows. This is the framework that functions like chord changes of a jazz chart to help you draft your own version of a script for your students.

I already identified the purpose of each step for you next to each step number and gave you an example of the words

141

I use with my students to serve that purpose. As you look at each purpose statement and my script, imagine how you would talk to your students if you were trying to get them to accomplish whatever is in the purpose statement. For example, the first purpose statement identifies what the students should be able to do within the first ten seconds of our routine: physically settling in. How will you cue your students to do this so that it becomes an automatic response for them to physically prepare their bodies for what you want them to do? I simply turn off the lights and say, "I invite you to bring your body to stillness and get comfortable." In less than ten seconds, my students have gone from wiggling and chatting to being silent and comfortable in their space. It didn't happen the first time I asked them to do it, but every time we practiced it, more and more of them began responding more and more quickly, and now it's an automatic response for them to be still and relax in my presence. Ahhh... it's lovely.

I suggest going through each step and thinking about what you currently do to help your students achieve each purpose statement. What do you do that already works? How can you continue to incorporate what already works for you into this process? What steps do you not currently do on a daily basis? How do you think adding those steps into your daily routine will help your students better meet your expectations as musicians and as students?

Go through this. Be willing to try something that won't be perfect. Be willing to try things that feel awkward. Be willing to grow. You ask your students to try new things, take new risks, and perform in front of others. This is your chance to model the process of learning a new skill, practicing it, and reaping the benefits.

If you are hesitant to take this step and decide you're going to wing it, then don't be surprised when you find yourself saying, "This didn't work." It won't work anymore than the most exquisite piano will play *Rhapsody in Blue* if a non-pianist sits at the keyboard. It can only do that if there is a human being who took the time to study it, understand it, practice it, and re-practice it until she can sit at the keyboard and make it effortlessly come alive as beautiful music because every muscle in her body was trained to recreate that music on demand.

That's what you are doing with this process. You are training your students' brains and bodies to get into the physical and mental space they need to be in to turn their instruments into extensions of themselves and tune into band as active participants who are engaged in your rehearsals. Physics explains why there are so many musical benefits from this process. All you have to do is care enough about achieving your goals that you do whatever it takes to use this process to help you be the best teacher you can be and watch as your stress levels become manageable and your students take ownership of their own learning and behavior.

Because I am such a believer in this magical First Four Minutes protocol, I'd like to see it be successful for you. If you take the time to put a script in place and would like to brainstorm how it might work in your classroom, I invite you to click this link and set up a complimentary strategy session so we can help you make it a success: https://LesleyMoffatCalendar.as.me/

I will be happy to talk to you about your biggest obstacles and help you find the simplest solution for overcoming them using this tool or any of the other resources I accumulated over the course of my more than thirty years as a music educator. Let me save you a lot of time and wasted efforts so you can focus on what's really important to you!

You can download a free pdf of this template at TheFirstFourMinutes.com

First Four Minutes Template: Tuning in for Band

STEP ONE: *Physically Settling In*
(10 seconds)

- My cue to the students that we are about to begin is the shutting off of the lights.
- Moffat's First Four Minutes:
  - *I'd like to invite you to bring your body to stillness and get comfortable.*
- Now write your own script in a journal or Word document.

STEP TWO: *Blocking Out Distractions*
(10 seconds)

- Reducing or eliminating visual distractions is a big help in getting kids settled.
- Moffat's First Four Minutes:
  - *As you settle in, if you're comfortable with your eyes closed, I invite you to close your eyes; otherwise, having a soft gaze is just fine.*
- Now write your own script in a journal or Word document.

STEP THREE: *Physical Awareness*
(30 seconds)

- This serves to bring their attention to the physical feelings in their bodies (which slows down mind-chatter).
- Moffat's First Four Minutes:
  - *Notice how you feel right now.*
  - *Can you feel your heart beating?*
  - *Is it fast or slow?*
  - *Notice if your breath is smooth or shallow.*
  - *How does your body feel?*
  - *What thoughts are coming into your head?*
  - *Just notice these things – no need to change anything.*
- Now write your own script in a journal or Word document.

STEP FOUR: Relaxation to Prepare the Mind and Body to Learn
(60 seconds)

- Once we've settled down their bodies, we can help them become less distracted and more focused by giving them cues to notice how their bodies feel when they do certain things.
- Moffat's First Four Minutes:
  - *As you breathe through your nose, allow the air to fill up your lungs completely each time.*

- □ *And as you exhale, maybe you notice how it feels when you release your tongue from the roof of your mouth.*
- □ *On your next exhale, notice how it feels as you allow the muscles in your face and jaw to simply relax and soften.*
- □ *Take a nice, deep breath, and as you slowly exhale, allow your shoulders to melt away from your ears, and let your arms and hands feel heavy and simply rest wherever they are comfortable.*
- □ *On your next exhale, perhaps you notice how your back, sits bones, thighs, and feet anchor you into your chair comfortably so all the muscles in your body can begin to relax.*
- □ *Notice how you feel.*
- □ *Can you notice your heart beating?*
- □ *Is it different than a few minutes ago?*
- □ *How about your breath? Is it smoother or deeper?*
- □ *Just notice how you feel.*
- Now write your own script in a journal or Word document.

STEP FIVE: Deep Relaxation and Restoration
(90 seconds)

- As their bodies relax, the energy in each individual as well as the collective energy begins to shift and settle. A palpable calm can be felt by participants. You are literally synchronizing your students so they are physically and mentally in tune with one another. Once you've taught your students to master this, life will never be the same!

- Moffat's First Four Minutes:
  - *Imagine being in the comfiest and coziest place you've ever been. Maybe that's in a bean bag chair, under the covers during a rainstorm, snuggled under a blanket by the fire, lying on the beach in the warm sun, or wherever it is when you feel the most relaxed.*
  - *What does that feel like?*
  - *As I count from 1 to 10, use each number to take a deep inhale and then exhale and feel ten times more relaxed than you do right now.*
  - *Simply allow your muscles to relax and follow gravity.*
  - *Slowly count from 1 to 10.*
- Now write your own script in a journal or Word document.

STEP SIX: Awareness of Self and Ability to Bring Calmness and Relaxation to Mind and Body
(15 seconds)

- Once they are in a state of calm relaxation, reminding them that they got there by focusing on their breath and that they can use this skill any time they need to relax reinforces the benefits so they look forward to doing it every day.

- Moffat's First Four Minutes:
  - *Now notice how you feel.*
  - *Is your breath different?*
  - *Is your heart rate slower?*
  - *Does your body feel relaxed?*
  - *What is the state of your mind?*
  - *You were able to physically change your body and mind simply by slowing down and noticing your breath. This is something you can do anytime you feel worried, anxious, nervous, or stressed to help you feel better.*
- Now write your own script in a journal or Word document.

STEP SEVEN: Invitation for Common Goal

(Flexible: 10 seconds to 5 minutes or more, depending on desired goal)

- This part can be used as much or as little as you want. When students are in this relaxed state, they are able to receive, retain, and reuse information they are learning, so be intentional with the high-quality recordings you share and anything else you use. This is a time of planting seeds that will support them in learning the things you want them to learn.
- Moffat's First Four Minutes:
  - This is an excellent time to do any of the following (recommend no more than one each day). This part can be as short as a sentence inviting them

to imagine themselves achieving a goal or be more directed by your cues, such as doing the following activities while students are in this calm state:

- Have them listen to and feel a piece of music for a deeper connection than they get when they are normally listening.
- Use a YouTube video such as this one to allow them to feel pitches in their bodies without other distractions. https://www.youtube.com/watch?v=AQ7bJuW_PDk
- Play a drone for a minute or two to instill a common pitch center.
- Invite them to visualize a successful upcoming performance so they get a mental rehearsal.
- Ask them to mentally finish this sentence: "Wouldn't it be nice if ... " for something they want to have happen today.
- Ask them to be extra aware of their intonation or blending or musicality or dynamics or any other focus you want them to have for the day.
- As them to imagine how good it will feel when they have a class where they get to play a lot of great music because everyone is focused and cooperative.
- The suggestions are endless.

□ You get to decide what to introduce during these moments – and on some days you might simply move on to returning to movement.

- Now write your own script in a journal or Word document.

STEP EIGHT: *Bringing Movement Back:*
(30 seconds)

- This step is really important, otherwise you'll have really groggy students!
- Moffat's First Four Minutes:
  - Once you've completed the step above, continue:
    - *Let's start bringing some gentle movement into your body. I'm going to count from five to one.*
    - *Imagine you are in an elevator five floors below the ground.*
    - *As I say each number, you are getting closer to the ground level and when I say the number one, you can imagine the doors opening as you float your eyes open and you step into the classroom, feeling refreshed and ready to have a focused and fun rehearsal.*
    - *5: Begin deepening your breath. Maybe yawn.*
    - *4: Start wiggling your fingers and toes.*
    - *3: Maybe you gently roll out your neck and shoulders.*
    - *2: Carefully stretch and bring energy back into your muscles.*
    - *1: Whenever you feel ready, float your eyes open and show me you are ready to begin by being ready to play.*

- Now write your own script in a journal or Word document.

STEP NINE: *Routine*

- In order to keep the focus (and calmness and quiet) going, progress directly into a routine that they can do without music (this takes time to establish) that warms them up and has them refreshed and ready to start class. Same routine. **Every. Single. Day.**
- Moffat's First Four Minutes:
  - As soon as students have brought movement back into their bodies, go into a short warm-up. I use the same 32 bar chorale every day (Ray Cramer's Lip Benders #11 directly into #10) followed by tuning.
  - We do the same routine every single day, so there's no need for me to explain it or talk. The signal that the warm-up routine has ended is when we tune right after the warm-up.
  - Following this First Four Minute routine, begin your class with a renewed and relaxed group of kiddos!
- Now write your own script in a journal or Word document.

Once you write your own script, record yourself going through it the way you plan to use it in your class. This will feel awkward and you'll hate watching the video, but it's the quickest way to learn if what you are doing is working the way you want it to. If you rehearse and record yourself before doing this with your students, then you'll be better prepared to do it successfully when you do it in the classroom. Practice reading your script and imagining how it will feel when your students respond to your cues and become calm. Visualize it in action. Visualize the results you're seeking in explicit detail. What will your rehearsals look like when students are in a state of mind and body where they are able to intuitively respond to music in all its glory instead of you having to constantly coax and cajole them into doing what you want? How will you feel when you can get your students' attention simply by raising your arms? What will it be like to spend time working on music instead of monitoring student behavior? How much more energy could you have if teaching wasn't so exhausting? Really understand how this will impact your life so you have the motivation to implement it and reap the benefits.

If you didn't already do so, decide when you plan to implement the First Four Minutes in school (write it on your calendar) and then begin going through the homework and practicing delivering your own version of the First Four Minutes on video. Watch it back and see how you feel about it. Listen to it while imagining you are a student and actually go through the relaxation process to see what it feels like to follow the sound of your own voice. Tweak it if it doesn't feel quite right. Practice how you will introduce it to the students. How will you get them to believe in it? What can you do or say to help them see this as a helpful tool rather than trying to convince them it'll be good for them?

If you're on the fence as to whether or not this is really it's all cracked up to be, I want to reassure you that it is! I taught more than 30,000 classes in my career and raised three kids of my own. I did a ton of research about how people learn and practiced and applied everything I've written about in this book. This particular protocol is the one investment you can make that fundamentally makes teaching and learning a much better experience for everyone. By getting back to working *with* our students' and our own natural rhythms and biological programming, everything becomes easier. Stress levels are lower. Teaching becomes much more about facilitating learning and less about managing student behavior and maintaining classroom control. Students learn and retain things at a much higher level. Their artistry is unleashed, and musicality becomes much more intuitive. If playing in tune matters to you, imagine what it's like when you help your students get their brains and bodies literally vibrating at a unified level – that is like getting their personal fundamental pitches in tune before adding their instruments, which makes it so much easier for them to play in tune because they literally feel the vibration differently through a relaxed body than they do when their energy and nerves are left unchecked.

Now that you're as fired up about this as I am, I invite you to go back and look at the homework you've done (or do it now) and determine if having your students being more attentive and relaxed and less stressed in your presence would help you and your students reach those goals. From what I saw in my own classroom and with my Band Director Boot Camp clients is that this process is valuable on many levels, from supporting the directors' personal health and creating a classroom culture that is conducive to collaborative learning to bringing structure that supports students' wide variety of learning styles and having a consistent routine that helps students who experience a lot of uncertainty and trauma outside our classrooms.

This routine is the great equalizer – it helps clear away the distractions so your students can be receptive to what you have to offer. Remember the pressure washing example? Your First Four Minute routine is your way of gently pressure washing away the worries, distractions, and anxieties your students bring into your classroom with them each day so they can receive the gift of music, experience the emotions that come from being part of something greater than themselves, and create unforgettable memories that happen through the magic of music education.

Chapter 10:

Coda

The previous chapters helped you identify the goals you care about, get clarity about what you want to achieve, and understand how success and failure are determined by the consistency with which you implement whatever it is you are trying to do. By doing the homework to get clarity with your goals and creating a First Four Minute routine for your classes, you picked up some game-changing tools for helping you run your classroom in a manner that supports student learning as well as your own and your students' physical and mental health. You have the strategies you need for becoming the band director you always dreamed of being without it becoming an all-consuming, energy-sucking job that leaves you too exhausted to be the parent and partner you want to be.

As cool as all that is, there are some practical nuts-and-bolts that can get in the way of even the best-laid plans. Things like managing inventory, keeping up with grades, planning field trips, writing curriculum, responding to emails, running fundraisers, hosting meetings, going to festivals, directing concerts, and a million other non-instructional duties can suck every last ounce of energy out of us, leaving us little to none in reserve to put into our teaching and parenting.

I'd like to invite you to check out my website, mPoweredEducator.com, where I share all kinds of free resources you are welcome to access at any time. The resources include videos and links to content I created to help you in the areas that I mention here but with much more detail so you can dive deep.

In addition to the resources on my website, there are some practical pieces of advice I want to bring to your attention. These are some of the keys to keeping your stress levels manageable so you can be that badass band director you were meant to be. It's not the stuff you learn in college or take classes in, but it's the stuff I learned through my own life's work. I share them with you in hopes that you can avoid some of the pitfalls and enjoy more of the joys of this band directing life!

Lesley's Top Ten Badass Band Director Tips:

1. Boundaries are essential.

It feels like we are being good teachers when we make ourselves available to our students and their parents 24/7. After all, doesn't that prove we love them if we are willing to help them at any time?

This was an area where I struggled for the first thirty years of my teaching career. I would get frustrated with the sheer amount of work I had to do or the fact that my phone was constantly buzzing with texts and phone calls from students and parents. But, when I look back, I realize I *encouraged* that situation because I was constantly making myself available and saying yes when being asked to have the band play at various events, do fundraisers, and go on trips. I was the one responsible for the long workdays, piles of paperwork, and overscheduled life, at least a good chunk of it. When I had no boundaries between my personal and professional lives, no one could tell where one stopped and the other began.

I remember the day a mentor helped me realize that I was responsible for either communicating boundaries or continuing to live with interruptions 24/7. Her name is Heidi, and she told me to write a cover page to my syllabus that outlined when my office hours would be, when and how parents and students could contact me, and other information that outlined how decisions would be made regarding extra performances and activities. I resisted. I was convinced that if I went from being available all the time to actually setting limits of when it was appropriate for students to access me outside of reasonable work hours that I would upset everyone and destroy the program. I thought they would think I didn't care.

I felt like I was abandoning the kids who needed lots of extra attention.

Then, I thought about the alternative.

Not putting up healthy boundaries was actually a disservice to my students and their parents. It didn't help them learn to be accountable for paying attention when I gave out information if they figured they could just call or text me later and ask me to tell them again. Accepting late assignments when parents drop them off on your doorstep (yes, that really happened) so their student "can get into the college of his choice" isn't serving the student; it's teaching him that he doesn't have to learn to be responsible or play by the rules, and that won't help him be successful in the long run.

Ultimately, I am reminded that boundaries serve as excellent teaching tools. By setting healthy boundaries, we teach other people that we value our own time and they begin to value it more, too. Boundaries give students parameters within which they can learn to function with much more success than when there's a lack of structure.

What are your boundaries? How many hours a day are reasonable for you to spend on work-related activities? Is it okay for students and parents to call your cell phone after hours? Are you willing to stay after school to practice with kids who need extra help?

You already identified your goals and priorities. Boundaries are the ways you protect the people, time, and things that are important to you. When you feel overworked, under-appreciated, and burned out, ask yourself if others were overstepping your boundaries or if you didn't have any boundaries up in the first place to prevent those feelings. Boundaries change over time, so be firm but flexible, and use boundaries as a healthy tool to guide you and your students and their families to do things that support your desired outcomes.

2. **Parents and other adults can be the most powerful assets in helping run a program**
(But keep in mind Tip #1 if you want to avoid boundary issues and lots of drama).

Nothing is cooler than having parents and other adults who enthusiastically join forces with you to help you run all of the components that are part of a successful music program. Not only are they helpful, but the relationships you form with families as a result of the activities that involve volunteers and helpers helps strengthen the band community as a whole.

Don't try and do everything alone. It's much easier and more fun when you have a group of parents and kids working together toward common goals like raising money for trips, providing water bottles during a parade, and putting together end-of-the-year celebrations.

Enlist the help of adults who have a vested interest in the program. They can be excellent at taking care of the things that are critical to the success of the program but aren't in your zone of genius, such as organizing the music library, distributing uniforms, delivering cases of water to rehearsal, and a million other things. The key to successfully having parents and other volunteers support your students and program is to clearly communicate what you need. For example, sending an email that says, "We need volunteers to help with a jazz festival," is less likely to elicit the kind of response you want than a specific message that says, "We need an adult who has been cleared to volunteer in the school to distribute fundraising items at school from 1:00 p.m. to 4:00 p.m. on Tuesday in the band room. All of the items are presorted and prepaid, so you won't have to handle money. Please sign up at this website." By providing plenty of details, people feel comfortable offering to help because they understand what needs to be done and will sign up if they believe they can successfully complete the task. If you simply ask for volunteers in general, folks tend to be shy about stepping up because they aren't sure they'll know what to do. There are some incredible apps out there for managing volunteer needs and signups. Use those to your advantage and make it a team effort to run a program that supports your school and community.

Just keep in mind as you have enthusiastic volunteers helping you that it's your responsibility to clearly define the boundaries of what is and isn't acceptable for them to do. There are well-meaning parents who can quickly overtake a booster program to serve their own child's needs if they aren't guided by a clear vision that keeps the program as a whole at the center of their efforts. Help them out by creating clear and appropriate boundaries so they understand when and where their roles end and yours begins.

3. **The F Word Will Be Part of Your Daily Vocabulary**
Let's face it, fundraising is a fact of life. Whether you are working on a budget with your administrators, raising money for your booster group, or having kids do a fundraiser to offset their trip costs, you're going to have to manage a lot of budgets and advocate for funding.

You'll have lots of folks who will try to get you to sell a variety of products. There will be lots of ways to raise money, and it can become a huge management nightmare to do all of the accounting on top of all of your other responsibilities, especially if you never had training in budgeting and finances and accounting.

Find a trustworthy person in your building (ASB treasurer is a good choice) who you can go to with questions. Understand procedures for handling money and record keeping. Find a platform that manages individual student accounts (be sure to check with your district to make sure it's approved) and keep meticulous records.

4. Work Is Love in Action

I used to think of reporting attendance and entering grades as a waste of time. I didn't always feel joyful when I had to go back to school for an evening pep band event or meet with a parent who was upset about their kid's grade in a class that "should be an easy A," and I'd go into those activities resenting having to be there. When a mentor of mine said the phrase, "Work is love in action," it helped me change my outlook and reframe my priorities.

When I'm doing jobs that make me want to poke my eyes out with a pitchfork (I really am not fond of all the accounting and budgeting), I remind myself that the work I am doing will make the difference between whether or not my students getting to experience something like a trip or new piece of music. This reframing of the purpose of the task I need to do helps it go from being another chore I have to complete to becoming a way to serve the kiddos I love so much. When I realize that my willingness to provide a fundraiser that requires me to spend hours doing data entry ends up generating enough money to repair a bari sax, buy a much-needed drum kit, or provide a scholarship for a student to participate in a band trip even though his dad died last spring and his mom lost her job and couldn't otherwise afford for him to go, I am reminded of the privilege of serving in this role. Suddenly, the task I found to be frustrating or boring serves a higher purpose. It's a mindset shift that helps me get through the tasks that used to otherwise weigh me down.

5. Some Days Will Suck

There will be times when you find yourself crying in the parking lot after a particularly difficult day, or when you are standing in front of a roomful of students who just learned of a classmate's death and you don't know how to console them because you are also grieving, or you worked your butt off all day only to come home to your own family and find yourself snapping at them because you're exhausted and then you get a nasty email from a band mom who is unhappy because her son didn't get the solo he deserved in jazz band. You'll wonder if it's even worth it. Let me assure you... it is! When you find yourself in a funk, have a plan for getting out of it – perhaps you have a playlist that transports you back in time or you can sit down at the piano and channel your emotions through your music. As hard as it is to accept, there will be days that make you question if you're in the right profession and if you're even making a difference. In those moments, step back and invite yourself into a place of quiet. Remind yourself of your responses in Chapter 4 where you identified why you wanted to become a music teacher and how you want your students to feel. Reconnect with your purpose and let that inspire you to keep going when it gets really hard and you will summon the energy to continue – and perhaps you'll use those moments to inspire you to keep implementing what you have learned in this process.

6. **People May Forget What You Said, but They'll *Never* Forget How You Made Them Feel**

This is the plain and simple truth. If you can remember this as the core of your teaching, everything else will be so much easier. When you help students feel good (which is what happens when you have a daily routine that teaches them how to relax, lower their heart rate, and slow down their breathing), they'll have the physical and mental capacity to do whatever you ask them to do because they'll no longer have resistance (which shows up as distractions, outbursts, and other actions that happen when people have unbridled energy).

It goes without saying that the emotions students feel in your presence (joy, happiness, love, peace) will stay with them long after the content you teach.

If you teach students to feel good through the sound of your gentle voice, their own breath, and the compassion you extend to them while you make music together, they will trust you and will more readily and automatically respond to what you are teaching them.

7. Your Body Is Your Best Friend

When you find yourself experiencing anxiety, feeling stressed, having a difficult time concentrating, or snapping at someone, take a second and check in with your body. Is your jaw clenched? Is your tongue glued to the roof of your mouth? Does your stomach feel like it's tied in knots? Do you feel like you're going to puke? Do you have a tension headache? Does it feel impossible to concentrate? If you answer yes to these or other questions along the same lines about how your body feels when you are in a specific situation, you can begin to use your body as a guide for knowing when you need to take a moment to step back, relax your mind and body (which can happen in as little as thirty seconds once you master the technique), and then tap into your flow once you reset it.

Did you know that if you reset yourself through a grounding exercise before eating that your body will respond in a more favorable way to whatever you eat? There's a physiological connection between the body and brain. When you are stressed, your body produces cortisol. When cortisol is present, your body doesn't properly digest food because the body is in fight-or-flight mode, which turns off digestion, so you don't absorb all the nutrients *and* the bad stuff you eat is even more damaging to your body. On the other hand, when you eat something at a time when your mind and body are in a relaxed and peaceful state (reduced heart rate, even breaths, time to thoroughly chew food), that same meal will be processed differently because your body is able to use its energy in the digestion process rather than the stress-induced state where the digestion process is significantly impeded.

Think about how you typically eat meals during your workday. Are you consuming calories that your body can't process because of your state of stress, or do you intentionally get yourself relaxed and calm before eating so you can nourish your body and brain and they can work for you? Have you tried eating the right foods, but you still can't lose weight? What would happen if the only thing you did differently for a week was do a quick mindful meditation to reduce your heart rate and relax your body before eating each meal, and you ate each meal without doing other work, surfing online, reading, or doing anything distracting at the same time?

By paying attention to the little clues our bodies give us, we can avoid big problems and keep ourselves in optimum shape. When we don't notice and take care of the tight jaw muscles or tension headache or notice how crappy we feel after we stay awake all night worrying about an upcoming performance, we can't do anything to correct the problems. They manifest in bigger problems that range from chronic muscle pain and stiffness to other physical and mental health issues that sabotage all your best intentions.

Your body is a reflection of your state of mind. What is your body telling you?

8. Trust Your Gut

There will be times in your career when something doesn't feel right. When that happens, you must trust your gut. You were trained to pick up on subtle nuances in music, and you likely intuitively pick up on other vibrations as well. If someone offers to chaperone a field trip and you have a gut feeling that parent might not be a good fit for your students, contact an administrator and ask for guidance in how to handle the situation before it becomes a problem. If there is a parent who is especially antagonistic to you and he wants to have a conference, but you don't feel comfortable talking to him alone, invite a colleague or other support person to be present with you. If you're being asked to take on more and more activities that you believe are not in the best interest of your students (like way too many evening and weekend performances), have the courage to speak up before the impact of these decisions causes damage. When something doesn't feel right, there's a reason. Stretching yourself and your students to the point where none of you can effectively balance all your responsibilities just so you the band can play at four sporting events each week isn't serving you or your students, so make decisions with facts and that sixth sense. It's there to guide you.

9. Have a Mentor

I cannot stress this enough. You absolutely must have someone you trust who understands what you are facing. Your role as a band directing parent comes with its unique set of challenges. Trying to figure out how to manage everything while you are doing all the work involved in running your program and raising a family is a daunting task. One of the best things you can do is find someone who has walked the walk, who knows how hard it is to physically produce a baby in your belly while also teaching full time and raising a toddler.

I remember when I suffered a miscarriage on a band trip. I had a three-year-old and a seven-year-old along with 150 teenagers on a trip in another state. The final morning of the trip, I woke up in my hotel room in a pool of blood. The next twelve hours were grueling as I rode across the states in an uncomfortable yellow school bus, got all the students back home, dropped my own kids off at Grandma and Grandpa's house, and had my husband take me to the hospital for a D&C. Returning to work after my own personal hell and having to pick up and take care of my own young kids and all those teenagers was overwhelming. I didn't know a single high school band director who went through this kind of situation, so I didn't have anyone to help me through the emotional and physical pain. This started a downward spiral where I struggled to continue to teach and do all the activities for the high school band program and be a mom while dealing with so much grief. My depression and anxiety started to rear their ugly heads during this time, and my struggles were real. I felt so alone. Without a chance to properly grieve, I had to work through my personal loss in front of hundreds of teenagers every day without the guidance of anyone who could relate to my situation and offer practical advice. It was brutally hard.

I hope you don't experience anything that extreme, but if you are a parent and you are teaching music, chances are good that you will experience a lot of stress and challenges as you put your heart and soul into both jobs. Having a mentor you can turn to for advice, brainstorm ideas with, and unabashedly steal great ideas from is a life-saver. If you don't have someone in your school who can serve in that role, seek someone out. Nowadays, we have fancy technology that allows people from all over the globe to connect, so do it! Music teachers love to help one another, so do yourself a favor and let another music teacher be there for you.

10. *Love* is the Most Important Part of Teaching

When you are beyond frustrated because a student asks you a question you already answered 5,436 times this week alone or the piece you've worked so hard on for months in class sounds like crap at the concert, it can be really easy to throw up your arms in frustration and wonder if what you're doing even matters. But if you stop for just a moment and realize that the student who asked that question lost his grandma last night and was understandably distracted when you were explaining something earlier, you can compassionately respond with love and patience rather than, "I already went over that in class, posted it on the website, sent it in a reminder text, and emailed your parents about this, so look it up."

When the 2020 stay-at-home orders happened, I decided I wanted to do a virtual band reunion and connect with students I had for the past three-plus decades I've been teaching. Who showed up? Do you think it was the "superstar" students? The ones who are now famous conductors, performers, and educators? A few of them did, but most of my monitor during that Zoom call was full of the ordinary kids. The trumpet player who probably never practiced outside of class, the alto sax player who was one of my students in 1989 and helped my husband paint our house one summer, the second clarinet player who threw up after every playing test, and dozens of other ordinary "kids" like them. It reminded me that the kids I teach in school may or may not go on to be professional musicians, but they do go on to become members of society who participate in and support the arts (so many of my former students are now parents of kids who are involved in music and arts programs at their schools). They remember their high school music classes as being somewhere they belonged; and, from the stories they told, what mattered the most to them from their experience in my classes was how they felt in the presence of one another and music. It wasn't the fancy trips they talked about, or the spectacular performances at Carnegie Hall and Disneyland and the Royal Caribbean cruise ships, or my witty sense of humor and engaging lessons. It wasn't even about the quality of our music or the awards we earned.

The things they talked about on our virtual band reunion that brought laughter and joy to all of them and me on that Palm Sunday during the quarantine were the ordinary things: the silly rituals we had in class, hanging out in the band room during lunch every day, and jam sessions after school. What mattered to them most was the way they felt when they were together. The process of making music and doing all of the activities we did together through our music community nurtured them during the most formative years of their lives and has had a lasting impact on them.

What we do is truly magical. It's so important. It's about much more than just teaching kids to play a bunch of songs. It's about teaching them to become the best version of themselves they are capable of being through the magic of music education.

It is hard work. But the tools in this book can make it a little easier.

In the process of planning and teaching and parenting and saving the world, please give yourself the grace you give your students. Treat yourself with the same kind of love and care you extend to your students. They watch everything you do, so be the best version of you that you can be for yourself and for your kids.

When it gets hard, come back to remembering why you are doing what you're doing. (If you forgot, you can check back to Chapter 4 and see what you wrote there.) Remember why you spent countless hours practicing when your friends were socializing, why you went to music school and invested so much time and money into preparing for this career, and what you believe your purpose on this planet is. Keep things in perspective. At the end of the day, it's all about serving from your heart in a way that sustains you so you can do this important work.

Chapter 11:

Fine

Throughout this book, you identified and clarified your goals as a music teacher, the areas where you struggle with excessive stress, and your vision for your professional and personal lives. You created a protocol for helping you and your students consistently have positive music experiences without distractions that typically drain your energy through the First Four Minute script you created. Now you have your plan in place and are ready to go. The plan was carefully designed and customized to serve you and your students. You visualized, practiced, and recorded yourself delivering your First Four Minute routine and are positive your students will benefit from this simple yet effective practice. Life will be smooth sailing from here on out – until it isn't. Because sometimes, teenagers push back when you try new things. Parents complain or administrators don't understand why you're not delivering curriculum from bell-to-bell. You get tired of waiting for students to notice results. It's concert week, or there's an assembly and fire drill on the same day. A million things will get in your way, and you'll experience times when you think none of this matters. That's when you'll be tempted to give up and slip back into old habits.

If you invested the time into reading this book and really taking a look at how you can up-level your teaching while reducing your stress, you know why slipping back into old habits is a bad idea. If I gave up on making this significant change in my teaching career, I would have slipped back into my old habits and ended up having to retire early from burnout because I simply couldn't sustain my health and career the way I'd been doing things for many years. It was much harder work to teach in a classroom where I had to actively manage my students' behaviors and when I didn't have a way to help my students get and stay focused. The mental and physical fatigue I felt at the end of the day led to unhealthy habits that made it harder to balance my job and personal lives. After a long day at school where I was exhausted from the sheer number of people I dealt with, I was too tired to plan and cook a healthy meal, so I relied on fast food. Instead of feeling nourished from healthy food, I sunk into a food coma and wanted to collapse on the couch after eating, too tired to cheerfully help my kids with homework or do anything meaningful because I was too wiped out. Then, I gained weight and felt gross. My skin broke out and my energy level was zapped.

The clear connection between my stress levels at school and my personal health were hard to ignore. I couldn't go down that rabbit hole again. As hard as it is to revamp old habits, it's worth the outcome. My decision and commitment to creating a classroom environment that supported my needs and my students' needs leading to less distracting stimulation and more focus allowed me to stay in my career rather than fizzle out and crawl to the finish line.

Being a band director is my life's work, and I have a vested interest in seeing other music educators have long careers. I truly believe we can change the world through the magic of music education.

Discovering and consistently using the tools I outline in this book saved my life and gave me the stamina to stay in my career for a very long time. I cannot emphasize enough the power of literally being able to reset myself and my students every day through our First Four Minutes routine so we are no longer functioning in high stress mode.

Teaching other band directors how to reduce the impact of the stressors that lead to burnout, exhaustion, illness, aches and pains, and taking time away from their families is my way of teaching teachers the skills they need to be the teacher-parent-counselor-advisor-nurse-fundraiser-cheerleader-psychiatrist badass band director they dream of being.

When I wanted to fast-track my first book from an idea into a published book, I thought about a million different ways I could do it. But I had never written, edited, published, or promoted a book before, so I didn't even know where to start. I had lots of ideas for *what* to write, just like you might have lots of ideas of what you'd like your program and family life to be like. The big challenge was figuring out what steps to take to achieve my goals and how to follow through when things got hard.

Actually getting the results I wanted in less than a year instead of dragging the process out over a period of several years happened because I found a trusted mentor who successfully went through the book writing and publishing process before, taught others how to write and publish their books, and was able to guide me through it. The same principle holds true for you: If you want to build up your program without it taking over your life, the best way to do it is to find someone who's successfully done what you want to do and get her help. Just like taking lessons on your instrument with a private coach helped you master playing your instrument, working with a mentor or coach on the art of being a badass band director helps you bypass a lot of trial and error and get to lasting results.

Now that I discovered how to find a reasonable balance between all the different areas of my life, I want to provide the tools for other music teachers to find the joy that comes with loving the job and losing the stress. It makes teaching easier, more effective, and more fun for everyone when you have students who are able to transform from unruly and restless when they walk into your classroom to calm and focused. They behave better. They learn more. They are more engaged. You are less stressed. You get to teach instead of actively managing their behavior. You get lots more music and a lot less wasted time.

Once you master the art of teaching students to "tune in" for band, the sky's the limit! You'll be amazed as you watch their progress. They will soar to new heights musically as their bodies and brains become more attuned to their instruments. When you literally sync them as a group at the beginning of class, they physiologically reset to a state where they are ready to learn.

As epic as all the changes to my personal life and band directing role have been, I was hesitant to share my unbridled enthusiasm with others because it seemed too good to be true. I thought maybe it was just a fluke that my kids' behaviors, musicianship, and rehearsal skills drastically improved. I couldn't be sure this would work anywhere else until I saw how it worked in other situations, so I began to share it with colleagues. When it had awesome results with their classes, I knew I needed to see how it worked outside our school, so I began teaching this process in Band Director Boot Camp. I can tell you that *every director who designed and implemented their own First Four Minutes plan saw stellar results*! If you follow the steps outlined in this book, you can experience these same kinds of results in your classroom.

Everything I do with my students during our First Four Minutes routine is based on science. Through the simple tools of breathing and taking cues from me, my students are able to do the equivalent of rebooting their bodies and brains for band.

There's a great video on YouTube that has thirty-two old-school metronomes on a table. Each of them is randomly started. At first, they are all going at different speeds, but in the course of the four-minute video, the metronomes gradually synchronize and eventually end up moving at the same speed at the same time. The top picture was taken about thirty seconds into the video. Notice how the metronome arms are in different places. At three minutes and thirty seconds, you can see how all of the metronomes are now moving in sync. It's just physics. In the same way the sound and air waves take the randomly moving metronomes and unify them into moving in unison, so goes your students and their energy.

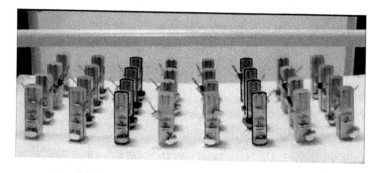

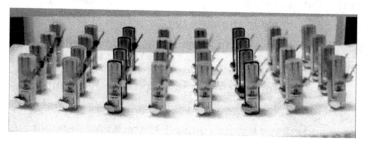

As your students enter your classroom, it's often with unbridled energy, residual anger from an argument with a friend, excitement from good news, stress from a test they just took, peer pressure to do something they don't want to do, or any of a million other distractions. When you have the ability to help them harness that energy and then defuse anything that could set them off or distract them during class, you found the secret power of being a teacher who actually gets to teach content and shape these little humans into artists who can work together toward common goals instead of spending your time and efforts keeping them quiet, refocusing them, repeating what you already told them twenty-four times, and wishing it could be different.

The skills they learn through your daily First Four Minutes routine help them tune their bodies and minds, synchronize their vibrations, and get them calm and attentive in your presence. You'll see it decrease stress and anxiety for you and your students, even the kids who drive you crazy! Like participants in Band Director Boot Camp said over and over, *this one upgrade in your teaching practice will take the headache of classroom management off of you and give your students the tools they need to responsibly manage their own learning and behavior*. It's frickin' amazing!

If you are thinking about how you can shift your classroom into a place where you can teach with ease and have time and energy left for yourself, then I want to encourage you to take the first steps.

Before you go into your classroom and announce that your students are supposed to close their eyes, breathe, and relax and then expect things to suddenly be different, you'll want to think about how you're going to make the changes.

Think about a time you went to professional development and heard about a great idea and then went into your classroom and tried it. Did it work? If so, what did you do to ensure you had a solid implementation plan in place and how did you work through the resistance you or the students had when it got "boring" or you got "too busy?"

If it didn't work, think about why that might be. Did *you* have a solid reason for introducing the new concept (did you *care*) or did you just want to try an activity that seemed fun? Were you *clear* in your own mind and when communicating to your students about what your reason for doing this new activity was and what your goal was with it? Were you *committed* to making sure it was successful enough to keep going even when it got tough?

As you plan how you will design and implement a new plan that will serve you and your students, take the time to really make sure you believe in it on a personal level. If you try to convince your students that this is a really good idea, but you don't practice it in your own life, it'll be a hard sell. It'd be like having a teacher who wasn't a very good musician teaching band. If that teacher didn't practice enough to be proficient on her own instrument, then she doesn't have any business teaching someone else how to excel as a musician. She must first demonstrate she understands how to *be* a musician before she can teach musicians.

Same thing holds true for this: if you are going to convince a bunch of teenagers to do something as "crazy" as breathing, you'll need to be fully vested and practice the skill of relaxing and resetting yourself so you can teach others how to do it.

So, practice – just like you would if you were going to build a new skill on your instrument. Practice talking through your routine and record it so you can hear how it sounds. As you listen to it (which feels *really* awkward), listen as if you were one of your students and be curious about how the student would respond. You know your kids best and know what will work and what won't. As long as you are authentic, the kids will sense it and respond accordingly.

I can tell you for sure that it's better to be authentic than to try and fake it. If you don't believe 100 percent that this is going to work but you try to convince your students to buy-in, they'll immediately sense your lack of sincerity and it'll be a hot mess.

If you really want a long-term solution that fundamentally changes how your classes operate, how much stress you experience, and how productive your students are, then this is it.

Here's a link to an example of what I do in my classroom. https://youtu.be/aHhYJPQvbkI It will give you an idea of what the First Four Minutes routine can look like, but your actual process will be unique to fit your situation. Use the framework and information in Chapter 9 to help you create a customized routine for you to use in your classes.

So, now what? If you didn't do so already, then I invite you to head back to Chapter 4 and begin working your way through the exercises in this book. Approach this just like when you were learning your instrument. Think of this book as the Arbans or Rubank Method Books. It has all the content and exercises you need to do in order to build your teaching chops.

If you did all the exercises and are ready to up-level your teaching and decrease your stress levels, your next step is to make a plan and then begin following it. It will become your roadmap, or your "score," for guiding you through the transformation on both a personal and professional level. Move ahead knowing that as you and your students begin to make time to reset your brains and bodies before each class, the investment will bring great results. It may take time and tweaking, but that's not a big deal for you. After all, you are a music teacher. You can adapt your routine as your needs change because you'll understand the purpose and stay the course. You are used to encouraging and guiding students through hard things because you know the value of mastery. I promise you that there's no better time than now to invest in actions that will have a positive impact on your stress, and therefore your mental and physical health, and your success in the classroom.

After the 2020 pandemic, our students (and we) are more stressed than ever and teaching will be even more challenging. Stay ahead of the curve by embracing the one change that will have the biggest influence on your ability to manage kids who are even more distracted, stressed, and traumatized than ever before.

All you have to do is follow the plan and implement the strategies in a way that works for your kids in your school and with your personality. I promise it works – if you work on it consistently.

With you on the journey!

Acknowledgments

"Thank you" seems insufficient for all the people who supported me on my incredible journey. Without my husband George and our daughters Kelly, Meagan, and Nicole, none of this would matter. My life's work has been our family's journey, and I can't imagine sharing it with anyone else.

My original teachers, role models, and inspirations to pursue music education and parenting in the first place are my own parents, Bruce and Jo Caldwell.

Nancy Ditmer and Dr. Tim Lautzenheiser are the true trailblazers for my generation of band directors, and both of them were heroes and mentors through their decades of continued and undying dedication to exceptional music education and leadership. I thank them for being so gracious as to write the forewords for my books.

I'd like to give a gigantic thank you to the people who helped make my inaugural class of Band Director Boot Camp a success: Nick Novy, Julie Bounds, Jake Bergevin,

Nathan Sackman, Ansgar Duemchen, and Tom Morgan, and to the directors who participated in the initial cohorts: Chelsey Eisenhauer, Shirla Wells, JDW, and Jill Rizzo. Thanks for trusting me as I got this program off the ground!

I am forever grateful to the community of people and businesses who have gone the extra mile to help me share my message as they continue to support music education, music students, and music educators across the United States and beyond: Dr, Andrea Pelloquin and JW Pepper, Danielle Winkler and Charms / Vanco, The National Association for Music Education (NAfME), Western International Band Clinic (WIBC), State Music Education Associations, Bill Kennelly and Kennelly Keys Music, Elisa Janson-Jones and International Music Education Summit, Dr. Matthew Arau of Upbeat Global, and the inspiring music teachers I've met through FB groups – Sara Iannelli, Sarah Nietupski, and Amanda Leigh Crawford.

A huge thank you goes out to The Author Incubator and the incredible team that made it possible for me to take two books from idea to done in under eighteen months! Angela Lauria, Bethany Davis, and the rest of the team are magical!

Thank You

I want to offer a personal thank you to you for getting this book. As a gift from one fellow badass band director to another, I have a special offer for you.

If you are someone who likes to get results without all the trial, error, and time it takes to learn on your own, I want to invite you to reach out to me and share your story. I'd love to know what your goals are and help you discover your biggest obstacle and the quickest way for you to move through it.

I can help you design a plan *and* a successful way to implement it so you can build the music program you dreamed of building, change kids' lives through the magic of music education, and be healthy and happy enough to enjoy it all! After all, isn't that why you became a band director in the first place?

There's no obligation to buy something. No sales pressure. Just a conversation to see how you can implement the ideas in this book to upgrade your music program and your life sooner! Schedule your appointment here: https://LesleyMoffatCalendar.as.me/

With you on the journey!

About the Author

Prior to writing *Love the Job, Lose the* Stress, Lesley Moffat's first book, *I Love My Job but It's Killing Me: The Teacher's Guide to Conquering Chronic Stress and Sickness,* explored her story of overcoming the myriad health issues she faced for decades as a high school band director and resonated with teachers all over the world.

Lesley considers it a personal triumph to overcome personal health issues that were the result of being an exhausted and worn-out band director who was on the verge of walking away from the career she loved. The responsibility, time, and energy it took to run her music program left her struggling to balance her career with her family life. In order to stay in the job without continuing to struggle with burning the candle at both ends, she set out to figure out how she could be both the mom and the badass band director she always dreamed of being.

Through the course of her own research, what she learned through trial and error, activities she used in teaching more than 30,000 classes, and her experience with how students learn best, she created a simple yet brilliant protocol that has the potential to change how teachers teach and students learn.

Lesley worked with thousands of people, helping them not only achieve musical goals (including repeated performances at Carnegie Hall, Disney Theme Parks, Royal Caribbean cruise ships, and competitions and festivals all over the U.S. and Canada), but also teaching them how to develop the long-term life skills they need to help them achieve their goals.

Lesley was a presenter at the National Association for Music Education (NAfME) and WMEA Conferences, State Music Conferences all over the U.S., served on the board for the Mount Pilchuck Music Educators Association, was an adjudicator and guest conductor in the Pacific Northwest, and is a frequent guest on worldwide education and music education podcasts and webinars, sharing strategies from her personal and professional struggles and triumphs.

The founder of The mPowered Music Educator Academy, Lesley runs Band Director Boot Camp, a program for music educators all over the world who want to build successful programs without burning out.

Lesley lives in the same Seattle suburb where she's taught for most of her career, developing relationships with students and their families as their teacher and also as a fellow member of the community.

After completing her undergraduate degree at Indiana University, she returned to her roots and moved back to the Pacific Northwest, where she and her husband George raised their three daughters, all of whom were students in her high school band program. Fun fact: Lesley, George, all three of their daughters, and Lesley's dad have performed at Carnegie Hall.

CPSIA information can be obtained
at www.ICGtesting.com
Printed in the USA
LVHW051657270122
709554LV00009B/562